what's going to happen to me?

what's going to happen to me?

when parents separate or divorce

by Eda LeShan

illustrations by Richard Cuffari

ALADDIN BOOKS
Macmillan Publishing Company   New York

— ACKNOWLEDGMENTS —

I would like to express my thanks to the following people for reading the manuscript and making helpful suggestions: Margo Howard, Stefan Janis, Ann Kliman, and Phyllis Wender. I would also like to thank William Hooks of the Bank Street College of Education for help with the bibliography. And finally, my deep gratitude to David Reuther, for being the kind of editor writers dream about but are seldom lucky enough to find.

Text copyright © 1978 by Eda LeShan

Illustrations copyright © 1978 by Scholastic Magazines, Inc.

Aladdin Books

Macmillan Publishing Company

866 Third Avenue, New York, NY 10022

Collier Macmillan Canada, Inc.

First Aladdin Books edition 1986

Printed in the United States of America

A hardcover edition of *What's Going to Happen to Me?* is available from Four Winds Press, Macmillan Publishing Company.

10 9 8 7 6 5 4 3 2

Library of Congress Cataloging in Publication Data

LeShan, Eda J.
What's going to happen to me?
Bibliography: p.
Summary: Explores the feelings and problems common to the experience of divorce.
1. Divorce—United States—Juvenile literature.
2. Children of divorced parents—United States—Juvenile literature.   3. Divorced parents—United States—Juvenile literature.   [1. Divorce]   I. Cuffari, Richard, ill.   II. Title.
HQ834.L45   1986   306.8'9   86-10769
ISBN 0-689-71093-3 (pbk.)

For my father, Max Grossman
—a lawyer who taught me that human
relationships are more important than legal procedures

contents

— INTRODUCTION —

Over one million marriages end in divorce every year. One out of every six children lives in a one-parent family. Divorce has become so common in the lives of so many children, that when one little boy wrote a fairy story for his fourth-grade teacher, he ended it by writing, "And so they lived happily together for quite some time." Many children growing up today don't believe it is possible to live "happily ever after."

When I was a young child I don't think it ever occurred to me that my parents might get a divorce. I didn't know anybody who was divorced. Today I can't imagine any child who hasn't at least worried and wondered about such a possibility. Chances are that you know many children whose parents are separated or divorced. In your class at school there may be six or seven or even more children of divorced families. That is how much the situation has changed in the last fifty years.

Perhaps it is a little easier to be a child in a divorced family if the same thing is happening to lots of other people. If you have many friends who have lived through a divorce, it is probably less frightening than if it were something very rare and unusual. These days, to be the child of divorced parents is no longer as embarrassing or unusual as it used to be. Today it is a common way of life.

But even if divorces happen to many, many families, it is still a very painful and frightening experience for each individual child. When it is happening to you, it is really not much comfort to know that it is also happening to many others as well. All you can feel—for some time at least—is that your whole world is coming apart. You feel angry and scared. You may even think that you must have done something terrible yourself, if this is happening to you. That isn't true, but that's the way most children feel at such a time.

Most children whose parents separate seem to go through similar stages in their feelings. At first there is a feeling of shock and surprise, no matter how long they may have known their parents have been unhappy together. This is usually followed by a time of being very frightened; children wonder and worry about who is going to take care of them. There are also strong feelings of anger at one's parents for allowing such a thing to happen. It is natural for children to also experience feelings of grief and deep sadness. Finally, there are many practical problems which come up—how to behave with one's parents separately, how to tell one's friends and how to adjust to moving, to living in a single-parent household and visiting the other parent. And often, just as children feel they are managing quite well, new partners may come into their parents' lives.

There are some things that can help you live through this experience and become stronger and happier. The most important thing children in divorced families need to do is to let themselves know all the feelings they are having. That takes a lot of courage, but it is the best way. If you try to hide your feelings, even from yourself, they don't go away. Instead, they get buried deep inside you and often interfere with your recovering from this sad and difficult time in your life. What hurts you the most, in the long run, is trying to cover up your suffering right now.

What I would like to do is to help you explore how you are feeling and to talk about all the normal and natural feelings that happen to children who are going through this experience. When you understand how you are feeling and how your parents are feeling, you can begin to build a new life. I hope that this book will help you to understand yourself and your parents a little better. Once you are able to do that, it will be possible for you to accept what has happened and to know that after a while you will be able to go on growing up feeling good about yourself and your future.

Eda LeShan

July, 1977

what's going to happen to me?

before

it happens

Right now it is probably hard for you to get through one day at a time. All you can think about is how angry or confused or scared you are, yet it seems as if most people expect you to go on living as if nothing was happening. Your teacher gets upset if you aren't listening; your grandmother gets angry if you yell at her; your father doesn't understand why you won't talk to him anymore; your mother thinks you are much too old to be wetting your bed at night or needing a night light. You may feel like it's the end of the world, but all these things are natural and normal things that can happen to a child when parents are getting a divorce.

The worst time for many children whose parents get a divorce is at the very beginning, before it happens. There are several reasons why this is often true. First, you don't have any idea what is going to happen to you. All children need to feel that their parents love them and want to take care of them. When parents are in trouble with each other, it seems, at least for a while, that they have forgotten all about their children. Nothing could be more frightening than to have the feeling that nobody will remember to take care of you.

The second reason why this is such a painful time is that, with rare exceptions, most children love both of their parents, no matter how the parents may behave. Sarah and Jim know perfectly well that their father gets drunk, comes home and throws things and yells. The time he hit their mother was about the most awful moment of their lives. And yet they love their father just as much as they love their mother. They can remember how he played with them when they were very little. Once he was a funny, clownish daddy who played hide-and-seek and taught them how to swim and ride bicycles. Now they can see that their father is a man who is very, very troubled in his feelings, and that makes them care about him even more. They can understand why their mother doesn't love him anymore, but they still do, and they worry about what might happen to him if they left him all alone. They even find themselves feeling very angry at their mother because she wants a divorce.

There is a third reason why the beginning of a divorce is often the worst time. Many grown-ups think that because they don't talk to their children about awful things that are happening, the children don't notice what is going on. The truth is that even little babies, and certainly children who are three or four or five years old, know very well when parents are in trouble. By the time a child is eight or nine years old, he or she is *very* well aware of how people feel about each other. In fact, the only thing worse than knowing something bad is happening, is not having anyone talk to you about it.

Lenny dreads coming home from school everyday; he knows that sooner or later his mother and father will begin to scream at each other. Sometimes it happens as soon as his dad gets home from work; other times they fight before dinner or while the family is eating. Lenny is so frightened and upset that he just can't think about anything else. As far back as he can remember his parents often have said mean things to each other, but this past year things have gotten much worse. Ever since his mother got a job the fights have been awful, and now he hears the word "divorce" more and more often.

Nobody tells Lenny anything. As soon as the fighting starts, his parents send him to his room. "Go do your homework!" they yell, as their eyes begin to blaze and their voices get louder and louder.

Sometimes, as in Lenny's case, the fact that parents are in trouble with each other seems pretty clear. In other cases it is very hard for a child to understand what is happening.

Julie's parents have never shouted at each other. They never show strong feelings in front of her. They are very quiet and polite—too polite. Julie just has an awful feeling that something is wrong. Her parents don't laugh anymore. The family doesn't go on picnics or to the movies or to visit people, or have company come to their house anymore. Julie hears her mother talking in whispers to Grandma on the phone. Sometimes she hears her mother crying in the bathroom. Her daddy doesn't come home for supper most of the time; she hardly ever sees him. He says he has to go away on trips almost every weekend, but he doesn't say where he is going.

In this kind of situation, one of the worst things that can happen is when parents begin to send messages to each other through the children. Mother says, "Tell your father I'm going out tonight and to pay the baby-sitter when he gets home." Or Daddy says, "I can't talk to your mother anymore. Please tell her that if she doesn't stop nagging me for more money, I'm going to move out."

– Is It My Fault? –

Right now, while all kinds of mysterious and terrible things are happening, it is natural to be confused or scared. It is natural to feel angry at your parents. It is natural to worry most of the time about what will happen to you. It is natural to wish it would all stop and everything would be all right, the way it used to be. It also seems to be a very common and normal reaction for children to blame themselves. They think: "Maybe my mother and father would get along better if they didn't have me to take care of"; or, "If I behaved better maybe all this would never have happened. It's all because I make them angry"; or, "I guess I am a disappointment to them; I'm not the kind of child they wanted."

But this is simply not true. When parents fall out of love with each other or when they have problems in getting along with each other, *it is never, ever, the fault of the children*.

When a divorce begins to happen, the one thing you need to be sure about is that it is not your fault in any way. Unhappy marriages have to do with adults, not with children.

– Why It Happens –

The reasons why parents may feel that they must separate and eventually get a divorce have to do with a time long before you were born. Sometimes people get married when they are too young to really know themselves or each other well enough. They may have had many problems growing up and somehow they thought that getting married would solve all their problems.

Some people get married long before they are grown up enough to understand how difficult it is to learn to share, to take responsibility for another person. Some people run away from problems they are having with their own parents and think getting married will make everything all right. Nothing could be further from the truth. Living together as a married couple is hard work. It takes great understanding, patience, sympathy and most of all, the ability to talk to each other about how they feel. Many people who are adults as far as their age is concerned are still not very grown up in their feelings.

Sophie's mother and father got married while they were still in high school. Both of them had very strict parents who made many rules and regulations, and all they wanted to do was to escape. Richard's parents got married right after Richard's father graduated from college. They were so in love with each other that they just felt they could not wait. In order to earn enough money to live, Richard's father went to work for his father-in-law. He really wasn't experienced enough to know what kind of work he might enjoy doing, and so he became a salesman. By the time Richard was born, his father was sorry he hadn't stayed in school until he could become a lawyer. After a year or two, he began blaming his wife; if she hadn't been in such a hurry to get married, maybe he would have stayed in school. He has forgotten that he was just as eager as she was.

Walter's parents thought they knew exactly what they wanted when they got married. Walter's mother was raised to believe that girls were supposed to get married, take care of a house and have babies. She thought that was all she ever wanted to do. Walter's father had been taught that women stay home and men go out into the world and earn a living. That's how they both felt when they were twenty-five years old. Now they are thirty-five years old, and Walter's mother doesn't feel that way anymore. She feels that she should have gone to college and had a career. Now she thinks her parents were wrong—that girls have as much right to use their talents as boys, and she has never had that chance. She loves Walter and his two brothers, but staying home all the time makes her feel trapped.

Jed's parents ought never to have gotten married—they just have the kind of personalities that are bound to clash with each other. When they fell in love, they each thought they were kind of ugly and not too smart; neither one of them felt that anyone else could love them. Many things had happened to them when they were children that had given them these kinds of feelings about themselves. They got married because they were lonely and afraid that nobody else would ever love them. Now, after fifteen years of marriage, they have had a chance to learn more about what kind of people they really are, and their personalities have become so different, that they just can't live together. Now they know that they are not ugly and stupid. They aren't shy anymore. They each want to do completely different things with their future lives.

The reasons for divorce have to do with all kinds of problems between the husband and the wife and in most cases these problems began a long, long time before they ever became parents. *Children are never the cause of a divorce, and children cannot save a marriage*.

Few children seem to believe this or understand it.

Kelly is absolutely certain that if she gets good marks in school her parents will stay together. John tries as hard as he can not to be so noisy and bouncy, and to do exactly what he is told to do, because then his parents won't feel tired and annoyed and will be able to get along better.

All children make noise, do things they aren't supposed to do, disobey rules, ask for things they can't have, want things that don't belong to them, fight with other children, have trouble in school because they don't understand what they are supposed to be learning or are afraid of a teacher. Children cannot control all their feelings and all their behavior. That is what it is like to be a child.

You will have quite enough problems for a while, without trying to save your parents' marriage. If they are able to work things out, it will be because they are able to figure out what they are doing to each other. It will be because they understand themselves and each other. It is up to them to decide if this is possible. It is natural for you to want to help them, but only grown-ups can save a marriage.

– What Can I Do? –

The best thing you can do is to try to understand how you are feeling and to let your parents, aunts and uncles, teachers—and any other grown-ups whom you feel love you and understand you—know how you are feeling.

George feels as if he is in the middle of a battleground. He wishes he could cover his ears because it hurts so much to hear the things his parents say to each other when they are angry. They say things like "I wish I'd never been born," or "I'll kill you if you ever talk to me that way again," or "If it wasn't for George, I would have walked out of here five years ago."

George is caught in the cross fire between two people who are unhappy. What he needs to remember is that when people are hurting a lot they often say things they don't really mean. Maybe he can tell his parents how scared he is. If, when things are quiet, George can tell his mother or his father how frightened he is, chances are they will be able to reassure him, and to control their feelings better. If he can't tell them, he might find comfort and help in talking it over with a sympathetic adult, such as his favorite aunt or his baseball coach.

Peggy hears much more than she wants to hear about how her parents are feeling. She wishes that there were lots of things she never knew about. She is embarrassed about the things they say. Peggy might be able to tell her parents, "I know you are very unhappy, but I wish you would talk about your private feelings when I can't hear you."

On the other hand, David is most upset because nobody is telling him anything. As soon as he walks into his apartment, he can feel the tension, but it is all very quiet. His parents hardly ever talk to each other, but he can feel in his bones that something terrible is going to happen. It would help him if he could let his parents know that he can tell that they are angry and unhappy. Usually parents have the best of intentions. They want to protect their children from being hurt or from worrying, and so they try to hide their feelings. David might say, "I know something is wrong and I feel scared and worried. Please tell me what is happening."

— Natural Feelings —

Sometimes when children are worried and frightened it affects everything they do. You may think you are stupid because you are failing in school. Or you may think you are just a bad person because you fight all the time with your brother or with the children in the playground. You may think you are a "sissy" because you are afraid of the dark, all over again. That stopped when you were about four years old, and here you are now, eight years old, and you need a night light. Or maybe you feel sick to your stomach before you go to school, or get a bad headache in the afternoon.

These are all normal reactions to tension and to worrying. When you begin to realize that you are frightened and angry and that this is a perfectly natural way to feel, you may actually begin to feel better. The reason for this is that keeping feelings buried deep inside is very exhausting. It takes lots of energy not to let yourself know how upset you feel.

It takes a great deal of courage, but if you can let yourself cry sometimes, and if you can let yourself think about how angry you are at your parents for not getting along, it won't be so hard to concentrate on things like multiplication; you won't get so mad at your friends and you may feel better. Headaches and stomachaches and being very tired all the time and feeling shaky or very excited and wound up are often relieved by being able to tell yourself: "I have a good reason to feel terrible right now, and there is no use in pretending otherwise."

Allowing yourself to feel your feelings is a step in the right direction. Another thing that may help is understanding that the hardest thing of all is to feel helpless. If you *could* do anything to make everything right between your parents, you would be much less upset. Taking action helps people when they are sad or frightened. But you are in a situation in which you must just sit by, wait and see. That is terribly hard for anyone to do. The more you know you can't do anything, the more helpless you feel—the more helpless you feel, the more you are afraid that something terrible will happen to you.

– *The Worst Fear* –

There is a special fear that all children feel from the time they are born until they are grown up. It is called "the fear of abandonment." It's a perfectly natural feeling for a child to have, since babies and children cannot take care of themselves. All of us are born quite helpless; if grown-ups didn't take care of us we could not live and grow up. Every child worries, at some time or other, about what would happen if he or she had no one to take care of them. Such feelings become much stronger when a divorce is beginning. The fear seems more real than ever before.

You probably can't remember now, but when you were a baby, you probably loved playing hide-and-seek with your parents or grandparents. The reason babies love that game is that even though someone disappears for a second, they always come back. That helps to take away the fear of ever being left alone.

When you were a toddler, chances are you cried long and loud when your parents left you with a baby-sitter. The reason young children cry when parents leave them is that they are not sure they will ever come back. That's the same reason most children cry and feel sad and frightened when they first go to nursery school or start kindergarten—or even later on, when they go to a sleep-away camp. There is always that fear that maybe they will be left there.

It doesn't matter how warm and loving parents are—most children sometimes have this kind of fear. The reason for it is really quite simple; children know that they need grown-ups to take care of them. They know that if they were "abandoned" they could not survive. When it seems that your parents may be separating, this fear becomes stronger. You feel help-less to stop what is happening—and you know you are much too young to take care of yourself.

One thing you can be sure about; *you are not going to be abandoned*. Your parents and all your relatives—and even the government—know you cannot take care of yourself. Grown-ups are not al-lowed, by law, to stop taking care of children. One or both of your parents will continue to take care of you.

To reassure yourself that you are loved and that there are many people who will not abandon you, this may be a good time to spend a week visiting your grandparents or a cousin who is your age. Neighbors and friends sometimes can be even closer than relatives.

Debbie loves to sleep overnight at her best friend's house, two blocks from where she lives. Suzanne's mother hugs a lot and makes Debbie feel safe. Suzanne's father told her, "This is a shaky time for you, Debbie, so come visit us whenever you want. We love you, and we know things are going to work out for you, once your parents get things settled."

– Other Things You Can Do –

Even though a child cannot save a marriage, and even though it is natural to be frightened about hav-ing no one take care of you, it is not necessary to feel totally helpless. It isn't even true that you're helpless;

the number of things that you can already do for
yourself, the number of skills you already have
learned, are really very remarkable. It will help you
to feel better if you do as many of the things you can
do as possible—such as making your own breakfast,
running the washing machine, raking the leaves,
cleaning the bathroom, doing the book report for
school, making arrangements for a car pool to the
ice-skating rink, going shopping at the supermarket.

Even cleaning up your room may actually make
you feel good, much as you have always hated that
chore! The reason it helps is that you are proving to
yourself that while you certainly need someone to
take care of you, you are no helpless little baby—you
are a growing person; every day, every month, every
year, you have more and more of the abilities you will
need to take care of yourself. It is much more important to concentrate on the things you can do for yourself, or perhaps even for younger brothers and sisters,
than to try to do anything about the problems that
your parents must face and deal with between
themselves.

– Mixed Feelings –

There are probably many times when you wish it was
all a bad dream and that you would wake up some
morning and find that none of it was really happening. These are such important and scary questions,

that it would be very surprising if you didn't often feel very angry, sad and frightened—sometimes all at the same time!

Kenneth sometimes feels relieved that his parents are going to separate. He just can't stand listening to them fight with each other all the time; he just can't wait to have it all over and done with. But at the very same moment that he feels relief, he also feels angry and sad because he doesn't want to see his family break up. He doesn't know which feeling is stronger. He feels very confused. Feeling two different ways at exactly the same time is called "ambivalence."

Another kind of mixed feeling is that when a divorce is about to happen, children feel that their parents just don't care about them at all. "Nobody really cares what happens to me," Gary thinks to himself, and yet at the very same time, he also understands when his mother tells him, "Daddy and I think it will be much better for us not to live together and it will be better for you not to have to live with two people who don't love each other anymore."

There is no question that it is very painful to live in the midst of an unhappy marriage—but it is also painful to have your parents separate. Even though you suffer a great deal when your parents cannot get along with each other, that at least is something you know—it is real, you have lived with it. Separation and divorce are mysterious; you don't know how it will be. Maybe it will be much, much worse. You know what it is like to live with parents who are unhappy together; you don't know what it is like to live with one parent and only visit the other parent. It is probably hard to believe this right now, but chances are that once your parents have separated, and as they begin to make a new life for themselves, they will be able to take far better care of you than they do now, when they are so preoccupied with their own problems.

– Many Kinds of Love –

There is another kind of feeling that is very confusing. When parents decide to separate, they usually try to explain to their children that even though they have fallen out of love with each other, they still love their children. Many children find this hard to believe. They think, "If a person can fall out of love with a husband or a wife, why shouldn't it be possible to fall out of love with a child?" The answer to that is that there are many different kinds of loving. The feelings of love between a man and a woman are not at all the same as the feelings a parent has for a child. You are a part of your parents' lives in a very special and important way, and that will always be true. Parents and children get angry at each other at times, just the way husbands and wives do, and there are moments when they certainly don't feel very loving toward each other, but usually such feelings do not last very long.

– *Getting Special Help* –

Because feelings can be so mixed up and can hurt so much, you may want to talk to someone special. You have probably heard of psychologists and psychiatrists, and special clinics and centers where people go who are unhappy in their feelings. As a matter of fact, these kinds of specialists have discovered that it helps a great deal if children can come to talk to them during times of crisis.

The reason is that we have learned that if children and grown-ups try to ignore or control their feelings too much, if they try to be too brave when they are suffering a lot, they often feel much worse later on. The wounds don't heal because they haven't been treated correctly. Let's say that you fall and break your leg while you are using your skateboard; if you are taken to a hospital immediately, if your leg is x-rayed and set, it will heal and be perfectly good again. If you try to ignore it and limp around on it, you will be in *big* trouble later on. Somewhat the same kind of thing is true with feelings.

Hurt feelings can't be postponed. In order to feel truly well again in the future, the best possible time for treatment is right away. Could you ask your mom and dad if you could talk to a special person about how upset you feel? You might be surprised at how glad they would be to help you in this way. Perhaps your parents are already seeing a marriage counselor or getting professional help. In that case you might say that you feel you need to be included. If your parents are too upset to listen to you right now, you might ask your family doctor, the school nurse, the principal of your school or your minister or rabbi. They would have to talk it over with one or both of your parents, but they might make it easier for you to get the help you need and want.

– Family Therapy –

In the last few years, something new has been happening; whole families are going to see an expert on feelings. "Family therapy" is a special way for families to find out about themselves and each other. Some families use such a program to save a marriage; other families find that it makes a divorce less painful and more constructive.

This is what is happening to the Connors family. Sylvia and Harold, the parents, feel that they made a serious mistake in marrying each other. They were very young and impulsive when they got married, and over the years they have discovered that they need something quite different for themselves. They want to explore their feelings so that they will not make a similar mistake again. They also feel very sad about the divorce and they know they need help. Finally, they have three children and they love them very much and don't want their children to be hurt by the divorce any more than is necessary.

Every Tuesday afternoon the whole family goes to

see Mrs. Marshall, who is a social worker. She has had special training in helping families. In the beginning the children were against the idea. They felt shy and embarrassed, and they hated hearing their parents talk about their feelings in front of a stranger. As a matter of fact, they just hated the whole idea of talking about how *they* felt, too. After a few weeks, though, they realized that Mrs. Marshall was a warm and loving person, and that it helped a lot for their family to try to be honest and open with each other. The divorce is still going to happen, but each member of the family feels stronger and less afraid because someone kind and understanding is helping them to live through the experience.

Someday this may be the way most families will deal with the problem of divorce. It seems to be the best and most sensible way. But right now, family therapy is more the exception than the rule. Most families try to deal with their problems by themselves. Or, if there is a great deal of anger, often they allow their lawyers to settle the problems for them.

Some lawyers encourage families to get special help, but others deal only with the legal problems— with what the law says about divorce. The problem is that getting a divorce has to do with laws and rules made by judges and courts. Many people feel it ought not to be that way—that when a divorce agreement is being worked out, feelings are far more important than rules. That is why in some states a family is required by law to consult a marriage counselor before taking their case to lawyers. Many lawyers are very concerned about how children are affected by a divorce and they are getting special training themselves so that they can deal with the emotional problems of their clients.

— The Worst Kind of Hurting —

Ellie would find family therapy pretty wonderful, compared to what has happened to her. One day, when she was eight years old, her father just left and never came back. She hasn't seen him for two years; she can hardly remember what he looked like. She feels terribly hurt. She is sure that she must have done something wrong, if he didn't love her enough to want to see her at all. She also feels very angry that he deserted her and her mother.

What some children have to face is that mothers or fathers may be so troubled that they just cannot be parents. They are wounded, deep down, for some reason that has nothing to do with their children. They appear to be adults, but in some ways they are still small children. Sometimes this is caused by a physical illness which has affected the way they think. Sometimes it is caused by very, very sad and unhappy experiences when they were children.

When Ellie's father was a little boy his father beat him and hurt him in ways that he never recovered from. He needed help, but unfortunately nobody understood him or took him to the places where he might have been helped. In a way, it was loving Ellie that made her father run away; he was afraid he might hurt her the way he had been hurt. The best thing that Ellie can do is to make the most she can of her own life with her mother and hope that somewhere, somehow, her father will get the help he needs.

Larry's mother hasn't been home for four years. His dad says she is in a mental hospital—a place for people who are very sick in their feelings. Now Larry's father is getting a divorce. Larry thinks that is a terrible thing to do. He keeps hoping his mother will come home and everything will be fine. He even wonders sometimes if his father or he caused his mother's illness. The answer to that is no. Mental illness is something inside the person. Many kinds of mental illness can be cured, but in some cases this is not yet possible.

Jody's mother ran away with a man ten years younger than she is. There had been fights and unhappiness between her parents for a while, but it was still a terrible shock.

Ben's father quit his job one day, came home and packed a bag and said he was going "to become a hippie!" He was tired of working so hard and taking care of his family.

In cases such as these, the worst thing Ellie, Larry, Jody or Bill could do would be to blame themselves. The best thing they could do would be to try to understand that it is natural to feel very angry at such parents and to feel deserted by them, but that these are people who never really grew up and don't know how to be good parents. Somehow when they were growing up, things got very, very bad for them, and the responsibilities of marriage and parenthood were just too much for them. Hating a parent doesn't help in the long run. As time goes by, and children begin to grow up themselves and to understand all the complicated feelings that happen, it begins to be possible to feel sorry for such people. There is also a feeling of great sadness because these children must face the fact that while their parents love them, they don't want to live with them—they just can't.

– In the Long Run –

Probably nothing makes children more confused and angry than to hear parents say, "We are doing what is best for you." That seems crazy right now, but more than likely it is true.

When a husband and wife decide that they cannot live together any longer, they know that separation and divorce will be very hard on them and on their children. Most parents do not take such a step lightly. It usually happens when they feel there is just nothing else to be done. Your parents believe that each of them will be happier people if they are not together. And that is usually exactly what happens. It takes a long time and the readjustment is never easy, but in most cases you will eventually have two parents who can give you the love and attention you need so badly, because they are leading happier lives.

Maybe, while you are living through these unhappy and confusing times, it would help you to think about what happens to most families where the parents stay together "for the sake of the children."

Beth is fifteen years old. She has known for a long time that her parents do not love each other. Her mother and father have terrible fights. Beth's mother is very sick in her feelings; twice she tried to commit suicide. Her father has been told by many doctors that it would be much better for everyone if he got a divorce and took Beth to live with him. The doctors say that the sickness in her mother's feelings is only made worse by trying to keep the marriage going. Yet both parents tell Beth that they are staying together for her sake.

Beth is miserable. She gets terrible headaches and can't sleep at night. She has trouble remembering and does poorly in school. She can't seem to make any friends. She feels angry and sad and somehow blames herself for everything that is happening. If it weren't for her, her parents would get a divorce. The truth is that Beth's parents are using her as a way of not facing their problems with each other. Beth would be the first person to say that this is worse than if her parents were to get a divorce.

Kevin's parents lead separate lives. They never do anything or go anywhere together. They hardly speak to each other at all. The house is like a hotel where strangers come just to sleep. Kevin feels as if he is walking on sharp pins all the time; he never feels really happy or relaxed. When he goes to a movie with his mother, he feels guilty that his father will think he's siding with his mother. When he went on a weekend fishing trip with his father, he worried about whether his mother was angry at him because he was enjoying his father's company.

Kevin is jealous of his older sister who is away at college. He can't wait to finish high school, so he can get away from this unhappy place. Each of his parents has confided in him that they no longer love each other, but they are staying together until he is grown up. The truth is that Kevin's parents are punishing each other because they each feel so angry and hurt; it has nothing to do with their children.

Margaret is twenty-six years old. She thinks she is in love with a young man, but she does not want to get married; she is too frightened of marriage. She says, "I lived for twenty years with parents who did not love each other. I knew they each had someone else whom they loved. I heard my mother talking to another man on the telephone all the time. My dad would go away for days at a time, and once by accident, I saw him in a restaurant, holding hands with a lady. They told me that they didn't believe in divorce when there were children. If this is what marriage is all about, I don't want to ever get married."

If Margaret's parents had gotten a divorce and had each married someone else, it is very likely that instead of knowing only one bad marriage, she might have known about two happy marriages.

It is easy to understand how Beth and Kevin and Margaret feel, but right now, it is probably hard for you to believe what they feel is true for you, too. If you're like most children, you worry and think a lot about what is going to happen to you. Which parent will you live with? How often will you see the parent you will not be living with? Will you have to move? Will you have to go to a new school, live in a new neighborhood and make new friends? What will happen if your mother has a full-time job? What would it be like if your father had to learn to cook and clean and shop and take care of you? These are all big questions.

You will begin to feel better when you have the answers to these questions. One thing we know for sure is that both children and adults can learn to deal with whatever happens; it is the *uncertainty* that is most painful of all.

It may be very hard to believe this right now, but you are going to be taken care of and you will be able to adjust to the new life that is ahead of you. If you're like most children, your parents' divorce will probably lead to your becoming a stronger person. You will learn that people do survive such difficulties, and, in fact, that facing the problems and dealing with them can lead to a happier and more satisfying life.

Right now you probably cannot imagine ever feeling happy and safe again. But you will. Not all the time—perhaps not even most of the time—but that is true in all families. It is very hard to think about how things will be in a few months and even harder to imagine how things will be in a few years, but soon you will know what is going to happen and you will be surprised to discover that lots of times will be fun and exciting and good again.

when
it happens

It has happened. You are probably living with either your mother or your father, at least most of the time. You know that life goes on; you eat and sleep and go to school and play. It seems as if many things are the same as they were before, but everything is really quite different. For one thing, you have had to give up hoping that your parents would not get a divorce.

For the first few months after your parents have separated, there are two things you can do that will help you to feel better. First, think about how you are feeling and try not to be afraid of all your mixed-up feelings. Second, try to accept the fact that changing is part of growing. Many of the things that happen right after a divorce will change a great deal in a short time. What may seem to be true today may be quite different in a day or a week or a month. It is normal to think that you and your parents will continue to feel confused and frightened, angry and exhausted, but it does not happen that way. After the sadness, shock and confusion, both parents and children begin to

find ways of solving some of the special problems a
divorced family has to face.

Right now, all you can be sure about is change
itself. That isn't a comfortable idea for most children.
You would like to know exactly what is going to happen. You wish your life could be very orderly and
predictable. The trouble is that if things couldn't
change, they also couldn't get better. That is something worth thinking about.

– A Time for Sadness –

When two people get married, they have a wedding
to share their happiness with all the people they love.
It is a time of celebration and it adds to the happiness
to all be together. When someone we love dies, we
have funeral services, because when people can share
their grief with each other, it helps them to feel better. A divorce is a kind of death of a marriage and
some people are beginning to feel that this event
needs to be shared, too. These families feel that while
the divorce is necessary, they don't want it to seem as
if the marriage wasn't important. Some good things
did happen; most important among those good things
are the children who were born.

Some churches have begun to do something which
is quite interesting. The ministers or rabbis perform
"divorce services," in somewhat the same way they
conduct marriage services. What happens is that the

parents and children come together to the church, often with their relatives and friends, and there is a special ceremony in which the minister talks about the end of a marriage; why it happened, how the family feels, their hopes for the future.

Maybe this sounds like a strange thing to do, but it is just as important to recognize the end of a part of one's life as it is to celebrate its beginning.

One such divorce service went like this:

We are gathered here today, in sadness, because Lucy and Robert have realized that they do not want to be married to each other any longer. They have considered this matter very carefully. They are glad that they met and fell in love and had two children, Paul and Ginger, who are here with them now.

Lucy and Robert want all of you—their relatives and friends—to know that they will continue to care about each other and wish a wonderful and fulfilling life to each other, and that together they will always love and care for their children. They hope that they will be able to work out all their problems with wisdom and patience and understanding.

Lucy and Robert wish to celebrate the happy years they had together, and to grieve for this sad thing that has happened. They love all of you very much and hope that you will continue to be very much part of their lives. They still believe very strongly in the experience of marriage. They know that loving is the most important thing in the whole world. We all feel sad today, but we also look forward to a happier future for Lucy, Robert, Paul and Ginger.

A divorce service makes a lot of sense to me. A marriage is a very important thing; when it ends all the people involved need a time for mourning, for expressing their grief. That doesn't happen often enough. Usually there is no opportunity for paying respect to something that was very important, and always will be, especially because children were born.

– Saying Good-bye –

Children sometimes find their own ways of saying good-bye to the marriage, to that part of their lives. Helen has a picture she keeps on her dresser of her parents at their wedding, when they looked so happy. Joan loves to listen to some tape cassettes her father made when she was first learning how to talk. She can hear her mother and father laughing and joking with her and with each other.

Sometimes it helps just to lie in bed and remember. Maybe there was a special and wonderful trip to the beach, or a long trip in the car when everybody sang and played games. Maybe it was a day when Daddy came to school and told the class about what an architect does, or one night, very late, when Mom and Dad decided the whole family should go out and have a pizza. Maybe there was a special Thanksgiving dinner when all the grandparents and aunts and uncles and cousins came and the turkey slipped off the plate onto the floor and everybody laughed and laughed.

Such memories may very well make you feel like crying, but there is nothing wrong with crying. Remembering is important. It is good to keep such memories, to think about happier times. There is no reason to try to shut them out and forget. In fact, trying to do that only makes it harder to go on with your life. Remembering the good things may hurt sometimes, but it also reminds us that good things can happen again.

– A Changing Time –

Of course, if you spend all of your time thinking about the past, you won't be able to go on living and growing right now. There are so many new things to think about. One kind of life has ended and a new kind is just beginning.

For most children, divorce means living in a home with one parent most of the time and visiting the other parent. That is a very big change. It leads to all kinds of new feelings and experiences.

Karen misses her daddy so much that she feels angry at her mother almost all the time. She knows her mother is very upset too, and that is why they both lose their tempers so often, but she just can't seem to stop herself. She doesn't want to do anything her mother asks her to do. She disobeys a lot and her mother punishes her.

Michael feels scared most of the time. He lives with his father, who has to go to work very early every morning and doesn't come home until supper-time. Even though there is a baby-sitter in the house when Michael gets home from school, he can't believe that his father is really going to know how to take care of him. His father never did the shopping or the cooking or washed the clothes or dishes; his father almost never went to talk to Michael's teachers the way his mother did. When he and his father sit down to eat together, Michael can't think of anything to talk about, and afterward they each go into separate rooms and watch television.

Kathy feels shy and funny when her father comes to pick her up on Saturday mornings. He *looks* like Daddy and *sounds* like Daddy, but she still feels as if she is going out with a stranger. They are both very polite to each other, but they don't know what to talk about. Her father seems very nervous and jumpy. He keeps asking her what she wants to do, where she wants to go. He keeps buying her all kinds of things that he never used to buy. Before the divorce, when Kathy went to the zoo with her father she had to nag and nag for Crackerjacks and balloons. He used to get angry at her and tell her they had come to see the animals, not to buy a lot of junk. Now, all of a sudden, he buys her stuff she doesn't even want.

Jeff talks to his father on the telephone almost every night, but his father seems very stiff and for-mal. When Jeff wants to complain about his mother making him go to bed too early, his father says, "I don't want to hear about that, Jeff. Tell me how you did on that arithmetic test."

Toby and Seth both wanted to go and live with their father, but a judge said they had to live with their mother. Their parents still can't talk to each other—it feels like a war is still going on. Whenever they do something their mother doesn't like, she says she knows they wish they were with their father, and that makes them feel guilty.

All these situations have one thing in common—they are happening because a family hasn't yet learned the ways to go on being a family after a divorce. It is a different kind of family, to be sure, but children and parents remain a family in many ways, even after a divorce. It takes a long time for both parents and children to work things out. It is natural for everyone to feel shy and strange and confused in the beginning and for quite some time. The important thing to remember is that families *do* learn how to manage better and better as time goes by, and a lot of the big problems that occur in the beginning do get solved.

– Custody and Visitation Rights –

It may help you to feel better if you can understand how your parents are feeling. What frequently happens when parents get a divorce is that many decisions are made before either parent is really sure what will work out best in the long run.

The biggest decision of all is who is to have custody of the children. Sometimes parents are very clear in their own minds about this; other times they are still confused and upset. Sometimes it turns out that lawyers and judges end up making decisions for the parents, because the parents are too unhappy and mixed up to make up their own minds.

Included in the plans for custody of the children is another big decision about "visitation rights." Sometimes parents are so angry at each other that they try to punish each other by making decisions that are not really helpful to them or to their children. If a mother is very angry at a father because he is the one who wanted the divorce, she may insist on a rule that he can only see his children one day a month. Or a father may be so hurt and angry because his wife has fallen in love with another man, that he may insist on a rule that the children may never go to their mother's new apartment, but may only see her at Grandma's house or in a restaurant or going to a movie or the circus. Unfortunately, sometimes when grown-ups are hurting a lot they make silly decisions that turn out to be very hard on their children.

What usually happens is that after a while when everyone calms down and has a chance to think about things more carefully, the rules get changed. Sometimes, when both parents begin to feel happier, they discover they don't really need visitation rules at all. They learn to talk things over and they realize that they must help each other raise their children even though they are divorced. Whatever may be happening right now is not at all how things will turn out later on.

– Joint Custody –

In recent years some parents who can, from the very beginning, concentrate their attention on what is best for their children, have tried to work out what is called "joint custody." Sometimes this means that the parents each find a place to live near enough each other so that their children live half of each week with one parent and half with the other parent. The children can continue to go to the same school and see the same friends.

Some families have found this a good arrangement. In other cases they discover that it means too much moving around for the children. They may change the arrangement so that their children spend a whole week or a month with one parent at a time.

Joint custody can also mean that even if the children live with only one parent, both parents have decided that they will make all or most of the important decisions together. That is an important idea. If it can't be done that way right at the beginning, perhaps it can be done later on, because one of the big problems divorced parents have is deciding what to do about discipline. That means who is going to be in charge of taking care of a child and helping him or her grow up in a good and happy way.

What often happens is that the parent who has

custody of the children begins to feel like an ogre. And the children agree! One mother said, "I'm the mean witch who has to see that Bill and Liz take their baths, get to bed, do their homework, clean their rooms. I'm the one who is always yelling and giving out punishments. Then their father, a knight in shining armor, rides up on his white horse every other Sunday, giving them all kinds of presents, taking them to baseball games—and most of all, listening to their complaints about me!"

Children know perfectly well that parents have to act like parents. It's nice to have fun with a parent, but it also feels very good to know that someone loves you enough to see that you don't eat twelve Devil Dogs and drink six cans of cola while watching TV ten hours a day and going to bed at midnight! Sometimes the idea of no rules sounds great—but not when we really think about it. Perhaps the time will come when Bill and Liz can suggest that they'd like to have some fun with their mother, and can tell their father he doesn't have to act like Santa Claus all the time.

– Taking Sides –

When parents' feelings are hurting a lot, sometimes each wants to make the children think that he or she is the good parent and the other one is bad. One of the hardest things that can happen to a child whose parents are divorced is being caught in the middle of a war going on between the two parents. Annie says, "I feel like a ping-pong ball. My mother tells me how awful my father is and my father blames everything on my mother. They want me to take sides—and I don't want to."

Annie is right; she shouldn't have to take sides. If she can do it, she might tell her parents how they are making her feel. If she can't do it herself, this may be one of those times to ask some other grown-up to help her let her parents know how she feels. Usually what happens is that gradually the hurting feelings go away and both parents realize it is unfair to ask children to take sides. But that can sometimes take a long time. One way to speed things up is just to say, "I don't want to take sides. I love you both." Sometimes just saying that much may startle your parents into thinking more carefully about what is going on.

A divorce doesn't just happen to parents and children. There are grandparents, aunts and uncles, family friends, neighbors, who can't help but be involved, too. If the divorce has been very unpleasant and the husband and wife are both very angry and hurt, other adults tend to take sides, and that makes it even harder for the children. A mother's parents may say that Daddy is a terrible person and they don't want to ever speak to him again; Aunt Sue says that if Mother didn't have such a vile temper, Daddy would never have left. Once again the children find themselves caught in the middle, where they don't want to and shouldn't have to be.

Again, this is a situation in which time is very important. Feelings will cool down after a while. In the meantime you can probably choose one person or several people who will be able to help you, without taking sides. One brave ten-year-old girl went to visit her mother's parents for her Christmas vacation. When her grandfather began asking her questions about her father, and whether or not he had been mean to her, Renee said, "Grandpa, do you love *me*?" Her grandfather looked very surprised and said, "Of course I do, darling." "Then let's talk about *you and me* and have a good time together," Renee suggested.

– *The Go-Between* –

In the first few months after a divorce, some parents feel they can't talk to each other. A mother may say, "Please call your father and tell him the furnace is acting funny." Or a father may call and say, "Please tell your mother that I am *not* going to pay that bill she sent me from the department store." When parents feel most unhappy and angry at each other, they may encourage their children to become go-betweens. Since the children usually still love both parents, this can be an easy pattern for a family to fall into.

Sometimes being a go-between can become quite serious; it can even include being asked to lie for a parent. Alice and Kim had just been out to a restaurant with their dad, where they all had a big steak dinner. On the way home in the car, their father said, "Don't tell your mother we had such an expensive meal. Just tell her we had hot dogs at the deli." Sometimes parents ask their children to keep secrets. Marty's father told him, "Please don't mention that Ruth (his new girl friend) was with us today at the museum." Sometimes parents may go on fighting with each other through their children. Andy's mother tells him, "I want to you to tell your father that if he doesn't get the roof fixed, we are going to move to a hotel, right now!"

At first, children may like being the go-betweens for their parents. They may enjoy some of the lies and the secrets. It also makes them feel important and needed. This is especially true in the very beginning, when children feel scared and are not too sure if their parents still love them.

Betty thinks, "My mother couldn't get along without me to carry messages back and forth." And Sam thinks, "I guess I'm pretty important to my father, if he tells me secrets." Being the person in between can make one feel very powerful and grown up. It can make a child feel, "My parents *need* me. I'm the only one who can keep them in touch with each other."

That feeling of enjoying being the person in the middle doesn't usually last very long. After a while, most children begin to feel uncomfortable and even very upset about it. That is understandable, because their parents are asking them to be something they are not—adults.

If you find yourself becoming a go-between, it might be a good idea to let both your parents know that you think this job is unfair. Just saying, "This upsets me very much," may help them to understand that because they are parents there are many things they must work out together, and that children can become very unhappy about having to be messengers or keep secrets or tell lies. If your parents cannot talk to each other, they need to understand that they will have to find someone else to help them through this period—a lawyer or a relative, a minister or some other grown-up person.

— Money —

One of the things that parents often argue about the most—both before and after a divorce—is money. That can be very scary because sometimes they make it sound as if there won't be enough money for food and clothes and a place to live.

What often happens is that when people are angry at each other, they use money as a weapon, as a way of fighting with each other. They punish each other by refusing to share the money they have, or by spending too much money. Sometimes they are so upset that they encourage their children to join them in this struggle. A mother will say, "You see? Your father doesn't care what happens to you! He won't even give me enough money to buy you new shoes!" Or a father may say, "Your mother thinks I'm Mr. Moneybags. She is going to drive me to the poorhouse."

Sometimes your father may say, "I'm sorry, but your mother is spending so much money that I can't give you an allowance anymore." Or your mother will say, "I'm going to buy you a ten-speed bicycle and a new football and a guitar," and you have the feeling that the reason isn't because you need or want those things—it is a way of making your father very upset.

It would be a good idea if, at such times, you could try to stay out of such "games." But what often happens is that because you are pretty upset and unhappy yourself, you begin to ask for more and more presents, more and more things.

When a person is not too sure that anyone really loves him or cares about him it is natural to have the feeling that getting a lot of *things* will help him feel better. Only it doesn't really work that way. After getting too many presents—or even just too many hot dogs at the circus—most children realize that getting what they want at the moment isn't really what they want at all. What they really want is to hear their parents say, "We love you and we will take care of you."

Children can often help their parents to understand what it is that they really need most of all. For example, Brian's father wanted to prove that he was still a good father. He took Brian to expensive restaurants and bought him so many toys that Brian didn't know what to do with them. One afternoon, after Brian had a bad upset stomach after a big dinner with his father, he decided to call his father up on the telephone. He said, "Listen, Dad, you don't have to treat me like a visiting king; just treat me like your son. Next week could we just stay in your apartment? What I would like best is if you would help me with my science project for school."

— Crazy Time —

Parents need time to adjust to living without a husband or a wife. Some of the things they do may be frightening to you. Pam's mother still cries a lot. Dennis's mother hates to stay home—she goes out almost every night. Kate's father seems to be drinking much more than he used to. June's father is so quiet, he hardly talks at all. Charlie's mother seems to spend all her time shopping with Grandma or talking on the phone with Uncle Lou. Some parents get angry much more easily; some act as if they don't care what you do. Some parents say things such as "Oh, I wish I could run away," or "Why did we ever have any children!" or "I just can't go on living!" These things are said out of anger or frustration, but they are still very frightening.

I know a woman who was divorced six years ago. She told me, "There was a time, right at the beginning, which I remember as 'crazy time.' I didn't really know what I was doing or saying. Now I look back and I can't believe the whole thing." This mother has talked to her children about those days and her children have admitted that they were very frightened. She told me, "Sharon says that the worst part of it was that I had promised her that things would be better after the divorce, and instead they were worse. It was a terrible time for the children, and I have tried very hard to help them understand that I was in a state of shock."

"A state of shock" is what everyone is in after a divorce has happened. That means that no matter how long you knew it was going to happen, no matter how well you understood the reasons, at first you still cannot believe it. The same thing happens to many parents. It has nothing to do with whether one or both parents wanted the divorce, or how right the decision was. Shock is a normal and necessary stage for each person to go through before they can begin to recover. If you understand that, then you will not worry quite so much about the things that happen in the beginning.

– Feelings of Failure –

Another thing it might be helpful to understand about your parents is that they probably feel like failures right now. You may be sure that when they got married and when they decided to have children, they believed they could work out whatever problems came along. Now they know that they were not able to do that.

The truth is that no one is a failure as long as he or she continues to try to grow and to learn from his or her mistakes. A person might be more of a failure if he or she refused to face the facts and went on with a marriage that could not possibly work out well. But often we *know* one thing and *feel* something altogether different. Chances are that your parents know they tried hard and know they did the best thing, but it still feels as if they failed.

When people don't feel good about themselves, they often do things they would not do otherwise. If a feeling is just too painful, a person tries to push it away in a lot of different ways. For example, Rachel's mother just can't face how awful she feels about herself, so she blames everything on Rachel's father. Deep down she feels that she is not a good person. But it takes great courage to face such feelings. Perhaps some day she will be able to, but right now, she shuts such thoughts out of her mind by being mad at Rachel's father.

One man told me, "I can remember as a child having to listen for hours on end while my mother told me that the divorce was all my father's fault. It made me furious. Much later on I realized that the reason my mother did that was because she felt too guilty herself. She blamed him because it hurt too much to face her own feelings of responsibility for their problems."

Peter's father feels that if he hadn't lost his job and if he hadn't started to drink too much, he might have been able to save his marriage. He feels so guilty that he just can't stand thinking about it. He's really mad at himself, but instead he yells at Peter. No matter what Peter does, his father always finds something to complain about, something to criticize. In some way that Peter's father doesn't fully understand, he is really criticizing himself, and not Peter at all.

– Unconscious Feelings –

It is painful to realize that your parents sometimes don't understand why they do things. It may help you not to be too upset if you can understand why this is so. The fact is that people have two different kinds of feelings. One kind of feeling is the kind that you know you are feeling at the moment that it comes into your mind. Equally important are what we call "unconscious feelings." Everybody has unconscious feelings. They are usually feelings that hurt so much that they stay deep inside us, without our knowing we are having them. These kinds of feelings can't begin to go away until we can know they are there and let them come out. Usually it is these unconscious feelings that can be explored when a family decides to go and see a special counselor.

Sometimes you can figure these feelings out by yourself. You may begin to notice that if you think about how angry you are feeling, your headache goes away! Or you may find that you don't seem to day-dream in class as much after you realized how sad you are feeling and have let yourself have a good cry the night before. When you let yourself think about how angry you are at your mother for not wanting to stay married to your father, it doesn't bother you as much to clean up your room. What you are doing is getting in touch with deep-inside feelings. The more both you and your parents can begin to do this, the better life will become.

– Testing Your Parents –

Even when both parents are doing their very best to take good care of their children, it is still natural for a child to worry sometimes. Living with one parent makes a child wonder what would happen if that parent got sick and couldn't take care of him. It is also natural to wonder if the job of being a single parent might be too hard. Suppose *neither* parent wanted to take care of you, what would happen then?

Sometimes children worry about this so much that they can't help themselves from testing a parent, to see how he or she really feels. For example, Janet's father went to live far away; she knows she will probably only see him for a short time during the summer. It felt lonely and scary to be alone with her mother—especially when her mother seemed so worried and tired all the time.

For some reason, Janet seemed to need to make things even harder for her mother. She never did what her mother asked her to do; she didn't come home on time; she left her clothes lying all over the living room floor; she argued every single night about bedtime; she took money from her mother's purse without asking. Her mother yelled at her more and more, and finally, after a long and terrible day, her mother began to slap her and hit her and cry, all at the same time. Her mother was so upset that she screamed, "Oh, my god, I wish you'd go live with your father! I can't stand you anymore!"

Afterward she and Janet looked at each other and they both got very quiet. "Why are you driving me to saying such terrible things and to behave so badly?" her mother asked. Janet didn't know what to answer and she began to cry. All of a sudden she said, "Do you wish I'd never been born?" Her mother looked shocked. "Of course not," she said, "I love you more than anyone else in the world. But you know I'm very upset, and yet you do everything you can to make things worse." "Would you ever give me away for adoption?" Janet asked. Then her mother began to understand what was happening.

Janet was testing her mother. By being as ornery as possible, she was trying to find out if her mother would ever want to get rid of her. They sat down and had a long talk and Janet's mother said, "No matter how much you try my patience, no matter what you do, you are my child and I want to take care of you until you are grown up." Janet's worries began to go away, and the less she worried, the easier it was to be more helpful to her mother.

– *Things That Happen in All Families* –

Guilt, anger, shock—feelings are so complicated! It is especially hard to understand parents at a time when they are as troubled and mixed up as you are. The important thing to remember is that many of the things that are happening now have little or nothing to do with how your parents really feel about you. Loving feelings may not seem to be there right now, but they will be again.

When parents divorce, they and their children often think that everything that happens is related to the divorce. But that simply is not true; married families have many of the same problems. It is important to remember that in *any* family children and parents have disagreements, get angry at each other, don't always get along. Lots of arguments have to do with problems all children have in growing up, and all parents lose their tempers sometimes. People can't always be considerate and kind to each other; we get tired or have a bad day at work or at school. We all feel depressed and upset from time to time. One of the things you and your parents will have to think about is which things have to do with the divorce and which things have to do with the fact that parents and children never get along well all of the time!

– *It Takes Time* –

Divorce may bring with it some changes in school and with your friends. If you have had to move to a new neighborhood or city, the first few months will be a very difficult time. It means getting used to a great many new people and new situations, all at the same time. The most important thing to remember is that you need to be kind to yourself! If you feel afraid and shy, if you have trouble paying attention in school, if you feel very sorry for yourself, those are natural feelings, and they will go away much sooner if you don't try to hide them or force yourself to get over them.

Some children feel so upset that this may be a time they need special help. In the first chapter I talked about the people and places where a person can find someone to talk to who knows a lot about people's problems. There is nothing to be ashamed of if you are having bad nightmares or if you feel like throwing up before school or if you can't seem to learn anything. These are normal reactions to a time of great stress. It may be a good time to ask a parent or someone else whom you trust a lot to find someone you can talk to about your feelings.

Even if you still go to the same school, things probably feel different. Sometimes your best friends seem not to care about you anymore, and you can't understand why. They seem to avoid you in school and don't want to visit you at your home.

The most common reason why this happens, is that your friends have a weird feeling that maybe divorce is "catching"! Also, you are going through a sad time and your friends may be too shy to know how to share it with you or how to help you feel better, and so they just stay away for a while.

On the other hand, there are likely to be many children whose parents are divorced, and you may find them being especially friendly. They know what you are going through, and so they are not as afraid or shy.

– Letting Others Help –

Some children feel ashamed when their parents get a divorce; they try to keep it a secret. Joanne constantly had the feeling in school that she was going to start crying any minute, but she never said a word to any of her teachers or her friends. This was a heavy burden for her to carry, and she began fighting with other children, and giving the wrong answers in class. One day she had a terrible temper tantrum in gym class and the teacher told her to go to the principal's office. Finally Joanne told Mrs. Williams the whole story.

It is a good idea to let other people know when you need help. That doesn't mean that you have to run around shouting the news to everyone. That would be as silly as trying to keep it all to yourself. But you know which people you trust and care about the most, and teachers especially can be much more helpful if they know you are going through a hard time in your life.

— *Only Children; Brothers and Sisters* —

If you are an only child, divorce can lead to feeling very lonely; there is nobody to share your misery with. It's true that sometimes it helps to have the companionship of brothers and sisters when you are upset, but it doesn't always work out that way. Both children who have brothers and sisters, and those who don't, have special problems—they are just different ones.

Only children feel that they are caught in the middle of all the fights that go on between their parents. And living with a single parent who works can mean spending a great deal of time alone when you need someone to comfort you. Only children also feel pulled apart when parents blame each other for the divorce. Many only children feel that things would be much better if they had some brothers and sisters.

In some ways that may be true. Having brothers and sisters can help a child realize that he or she is not the only one who is feeling so upset. Sometimes brothers and sisters can talk things over and help each other to understand all the different things that are happening. Brothers and sisters also may be able to stick together when parents seem most unreasonable.

But sometimes when there are two or more children in a family, it seems to make things worse, or at least more complicated. Dorrie has always felt closer to her mother, while her brother Roger loves their dad more. Dorrie and Roger fight all the time about which parent is right and which one is wrong. In Catherine's family there are five children. When their parents got a divorce, the children began having more fights with each other than they had ever had before. Catherine often feels miserable because now she never seems to have any time to be alone with her father. All five children visit Dad at the same time, and each one feels he or she isn't getting enough attention. She also realizes that it is hard for her mother to live alone and take care of them. It seems to be ten times as hard for her mother to learn to manage the five children all by herself.

Only children may find that for a while it will help if a good friend or a cousin can sleep overnight once in a while, and even go along when visiting a parent. It seems to make the new situation easier and more comfortable.

Brothers and sisters may learn that it is better to take turns visiting Dad or Mom, at least some of the time. One Saturday alone with a parent, once a month, may be more fun than every Saturday shared with a brother or a sister. Also, life will be much smoother if children don't gang up in favor of either parent, but try to stay out of such matters. Brothers and sisters eventually discover that the reason they felt so angry at each other at first was really because they were so upset about the divorce. Later on, as life begins to calm down and fall into a familiar routine, it becomes possible to be friends again—at least some of the time.

Some brothers and sisters feel the need to huddle together at first. They may spend so much time with each other that they begin to get on each other's nerves. But after a while each child in the family begins to move out again; each one wants to be alone with his or her own friends and do different kinds of things after school or on weekends. Later they may begin to realize that the more they try to be helpful to the parent they live with, the easier and happier life can be for everyone. It may be hard to believe, but the day usually comes when brothers and sisters can even decide among themselves how to share household chores so that they and their parent will have more time for other activities.

– Children Can't Be Grown-ups –

Polly is twelve years old. When her parents separated, she was so worried about her two younger sisters that she began to try to be their mother instead of their sister. After a short time the children refused to do what she told them to do and she realized the job was much too hard for her and that her sisters didn't like it either.

Trying to be kind and helpful to younger brothers and sisters is fine, but trying to replace a parent is an impossible task. For a while, though, it may feel awfully good. Jessie was pretty frightened when her father left home and there was only her mother to take care of her and her baby brother. Taking care of him made her feel less scared. After all, if she could take care of a baby, she could certainly take care of herself. It made her feel more self-confident and somehow much safer. But after a while she got very tired. The baby cried a lot and that made her feel very bad. When he refused to eat his cereal and threw up his bottle, Jessie realized that she wasn't old enough to take care of a baby without a grown-up around.

Sometimes younger brothers and sisters encourage older ones to become substitute parents. Hilary missed her daddy so much that she wanted to go everywhere with her older brother. She even pretended sometimes that Walter was her father. She wanted him to play all the same games with her and tell her bedtime stories and make her breakfast. For a while Walter felt pretty good about it; it made him feel as if he really was the man in the house. But after a while, he wanted to spend more time with his own friends, and not always have Hilary following him around. Children have to go on being children; they need the grown-ups to be in charge.

– Lots of Questions and Not So Many Answers –

There are many questions that one or both of your parents can answer—such as details about living arrangements—and then there are a great many questions that can't be answered, at least not right away. It is natural for you to keep on wondering why your parents stopped loving each other. It is also natural to wonder, even now, if they might ever marry each other again.

All children of divorced parents wonder if their parents will marry other people and what it will be like to have stepparents and step- brothers and sisters. Children can't help wondering what is happening to the parent they do not see very often. What does Daddy do after work every day? Does Mom think about me when she is working in her office? Is my father lonely? Is my mother crying?

Sometimes by the time parents divorce, one or both of them may have fallen in love with a different person. Or shortly after being divorced one or the other may begin to go out with someone else. It is natural to be very curious, to want to know if this might be a person the parent wants to marry, but usually it will be more helpful to control one's curiosity, for a while at least. Parents often aren't sure of the answers themselves. They are changing, too. Parents have a right to private thoughts and feelings, just as children do.

When Edward and Bonnie visit their father, they often meet a lady there who seems to be more than just a friend. They have the feeling that she may be living with their father, but he doesn't seem ready to talk about it. When people get a divorce it is natural for them to begin to see other people. Sometimes it happens so quickly that it makes you angry and disgusted. How could they get over the divorce faster than you can?

Actually they are not getting over the divorce that fast. Often they need to be reassured that another man or woman can care about them. Sometimes the loneliness they feel is so great that they just can't stand it. It isn't that they are forgetting or are feeling wonderful at all. It is just because they are hurting so much that they turn to other people for comfort.

life
goes on

After a few months or perhaps a year or more, sometimes it is hard to remember how it all began. When Leslie comes home from school, she rarely even thinks about the fact that her father won't be there in the evening. Every Saturday Vin wakes up and starts to get ready to visit his father without even thinking there is anything unusual about this. In some ways life seems easier and more settled.

After Liza's parents had been divorced for six months, she said, "The really *big* terrible things are over—like moving, and feeling funny going out with Daddy, and Mom bossing me around every minute. Now there are lots of little things that happen. Daddy forgets to call me up or write to me when he's traveling, or Grandma says mean things about Mom. The worst thing of all is that sometimes I can stop thinking about the divorce for a whole week, and then suddenly—wham! I feel surprised and hurt and sad all over again."

This is the way it is for most children and grown-ups. Some things settle down and other things get more complicated; sometimes it doesn't hurt so much anymore and then suddenly it hurts worse than ever. Each day seems to go by in a pretty normal way, but every so often there is still some reminder that everything is different. This is inevitable because people go on growing and changing and new things have to happen.

– Feeling That Nobody Cares –

A very common experience for many divorced families is that after a while it seems as if nobody cares anymore—nobody seems interested in what has happened. At first lots of people visited and called, trying to make you feel better. But after a while they go back to their own lives. Your favorite aunt doesn't call as often, your grandparents went away on a long cruise, and last week a teacher said, "Now look, your parents have been divorced for almost a year. It is high time you began doing better work on your assignments for class." Sonya says, "Somehow nobody seeming to care much anymore makes me realize that I'm not really so scared now, but I'm not really very happy, either."

– Others Can Help –

In some ways the worst may be over, but there are lots of little problems. Many parents find they don't have enough time to talk to other grown-ups. Most children miss having a special man or woman to spend time with. If you feel like you need someone to talk to, try going to parties or picnics or discussion groups with other people with similar feelings and problems. Getting acquainted with new people and finding new friends is often a big help.

Steve moved to a new neighborhood with his mother and for a while he felt as if he would always feel like a stranger. Then one day he decided he would like to earn some extra money during the summer, and he went from house to house asking people if they wanted to have their lawns mowed. One day he stopped at a house two blocks away from where he lived. A man came out and said that his own son mowed the lawn, but he seemed very friendly. He asked Steve where he lived and how he liked the new school. He said, "My son is eleven years old, too. Sometimes we go fishing together. There's a real nice lake nearby. Would you like to go with us sometime?" Before too long Steve felt very comfortable visiting Mr. Watson and the whole family. Sometimes his mother invited the Watsons for a cookout, and after the two families got to know each other well, Steve was invited to go along on a two-week camping trip.

Natalie began to have long talks with the librarian at her school. She had first gone into the library to ask if Mrs. Hatch could find some books for her about kids whose parents were getting a divorce. She was surprised to discover how many stories there were.

Now she and Mrs. Hatch are good friends. She has been invited to Mrs. Hatch's house for a weekend. Mrs. Hatch is a widow and her children are all grown up; she says that Natalie is good company for her.

It isn't easy to take the first step in looking for new friends, but it can be done. Sometimes a child can even help a parent take the first step. Marcia saw a notice in the laundry of her apartment building. It said that a group of single mothers were going to have a get-together in apartment 9A. When she told her mother about it, her mother said she wasn't interested in going. Marcia said, "Maybe you would feel better if you had other people to talk to, besides us two kids." She kept urging her mother to try it. "You're always telling *me* to try new things!" she said. Now her mother has several new friends, and Marcia doesn't feel quite so bad about moving from a house to an apartment building. "At first it seemed that no one talked to anyone else, but now that we've lived here for over a year, it begins to feel the same as the neighborhood we used to live in."

– When Others Take Sides –

When people get a divorce, it frequently happens that many of their friends divide up and take sides. In the beginning, when a person feels most upset, he or she usually wants this kind of support, and some friends feel they have to go along with it. That can be hard on the children. Sometimes a favorite aunt or uncle won't talk to your mother, and you feel as if that aunt doesn't love you anymore, either. Sometimes it may be your mother's or father's best friend, a person you have always been able to count on to help you and be your friend.

If you can wait a little while, many of these kinds of problems get straightened out. The first week that your family is separated, it may seem as if you are being disloyal if you call that uncle who isn't speaking to your father. If you call him two months later, or six months later, chances are that he won't be so upset anymore, and will admit that he misses you very much and wants to see you.

A few months after a divorce is a good time to begin to pick up on such relationships. It may be a good time to call both sets of grandparents and let them know things are going all right. Or it may be a good time to suggest that you'd like to visit some of your cousins during the summer. Parents know, deep down, that they ought to allow their children to go on enjoying relationships that existed before the divorce. Sometimes they overlook this for a while, but by now it is likely they are more ready to help you reestablish connections with people whom you haven't seen and miss a lot.

– Special Traps –

After many months, some children forget what it was like at home before the divorce. If things are going quite smoothly, they begin to think that maybe their parents could get along just fine, now. There are, of course, some cases where parents do remarry each other, but this is very rare and unusual. If things are going well it is probably because your parents are not living with each other anymore.

When Celia's daddy brings her home on Sunday afternoons, Celia pleads with him to stay for supper. Her parents feel embarrassed and uncomfortable; they would rather not become that sociable just yet. It feels wrong, but they wonder if they ought to make the effort for Celia's sake.

Probably the best thing is for them to help Celia understand that what she wants isn't real anymore, and at least for the present time, she should try to enjoy being with each parent separately.

Stuart wants his father to be invited to his birthday party; Elliot wants both his parents to come to the school play and go out for ice cream together afterward. Tom invited both of his parents to the School Fair without telling either of them that the other was invited. In his head he has a lovely dream that his parents would meet in front of the third grade's homemade fudge booth, and fall in love with each other all over again!

As time goes by, parents usually do learn to see each other without feeling terrible. Many parents want very much to join together for special times like graduations, birthdays, school sports activities, etc. So if parents offer to be together in these ways, that's fine. But if this is very difficult for them, it is kinder and more thoughtful not to push them into it. Most of all, try to understand that it is normal and natural to *wish* for your parents to be together again, but that this is not the way things can be.

If your parents prefer not to see each other, there are lots of ways of working such situations out. Parents can take turns visiting school. You can have one kind of birthday party at home and a different kind with a parent you visit. You might have special family parties with each set of grandparents. Wishing to go back to happier times is natural, but wishing for new kinds of happy times may be more helpful.

– Getting Your Way –

Grace has learned that it is easy for her to get almost anything she wants. The longer her parents are separated, the less they have any contact with each other. But Grace knows that both her parents feel very bad about the divorce and that each of them wants her to believe it was the other one's fault. Her parents compete with each other for Grace's love and approval. If she tells her mother that her father took her to the carousel and let her have ten rides, it is more than likely that her mother will buy her some new socks that she's been wanting. If she tells her father that her mother is going to take her to Bermuda for Christmas, her father begins to talk about taking her to Canada next summer.

It is not at all uncommon for divorced parents to compete with each other for the affection and approval of their children. It's an easy trap to fall into. After a while, without even realizing what has happened, children can find themselves becoming "great manipulators." It gets to be a kind of game to see how clever you can be, how much you can get out of each parent. The trouble is that it doesn't really make you feel better. The reason children find themselves playing this game is that they usually feel unhappy and they think that getting away with a lot or having a lot of things will make them feel better. But it doesn't work that way; after a while the game isn't any fun anymore.

Another trap is to get your parents to let you do what you want. When Edwin visits his father, he says that his mother lets him watch television until midnight on weekends. At home with his mother, Edwin says that his father never makes him have cereal for breakfast.

Sometimes when parents no longer live together they forget some of the things a child needs in order to grow up well. Taking advantage of your parents' forgetfulness can be fun for a while, but sooner or later it usually gets a little frightening. Children know that they need a certain amount of sleep and good food and not too much television. And all the staying up late and extra TV don't really make you feel happier about the divorce. For a while it may seem good sport to control your parents like puppets on a string, but after a while some children begin to wonder just who they are really fooling. And many children feel frightened that their parents aren't protecting them from their own immature judgment.

Sometimes a child can help a parent to remember this. Not asking for so much and not encouraging parents to enter into competition is the first step. It's asking your parents to make some rules because you need them. When you are grown up you will make a lot of decisions about doing things that are "good for you." When you are tired you will go to bed early; when your eyes begin to hurt you will stop watching television; when you get a pain in your stomach, you will stop eating potato chips. But there is no law that says you have to wait until you are an adult to start doing some sensible things!

– A United Front –

There is one part of being in a divorced family that sometimes gets more complicated as time goes by, and that has to do with ideas that parents have about raising children. In some families, neither parent makes an effort to agree with the other; in other cases, divorced parents sometimes have the idea that they must try to agree about everything or their children will be too confused. What both families are forgetting is that parents don't agree about everything in *any* family and that children learn some important things this way.

In families where the parents stay married, the children learn that their parents have different feelings and different ideas. Some mothers are always on time while some fathers are always late. Some fathers are very neat and orderly and some mothers don't mind a mess at all. Some fathers are very fussy about table manners and some mothers don't even seem to notice things like that. There is nothing so terrible about this; in fact, it is really more interesting that way. Each parent was raised in a different family and had different experiences, so it would be very peculiar if they grew up to be exactly alike.

Of course it does help if parents generally agree on the "big" ideas—about what is right and wrong, how to treat other people, and what it means to be a good citizen and a good person. It is very difficult if parents disagree completely on these issues. Nick's father believes in very severe punishments and his mother is very gentle and never even raises her voice. Nick is never sure what is going to happen next.

But some parents are afraid to disagree about anything. They think it is very important to present a "united front" to their children. Certainly parents do have to come to an agreement about such important things as which school a child should go to or which dentist or whether or not a certain beach is safe for swimming. But what some parents don't understand is that children would not really want them to be exactly alike. First of all, that is impossible, and second of all, then it would be hard to learn how to get along with different kinds of people. Teachers are all different, too, and so are other children. With some people you have to learn to be careful what you say and be very polite; with other people, you can laugh and joke a lot. Some people are very sensitive, others seem to be pretty tough.

A very important part of growing up is learning how to behave differently with different people, and to enjoy the ways in which people are each special and not like anyone else you ever met. Sometimes parents don't seem to realize how well children understand this. Kate laughs and says, "Daddy never gets mad about burping, but he *hates* bubble gum." Curtis says, "Thank goodness my mother isn't as dumb in math as my father is." Julia knows that with her mother she had better make her bed and clean her room or there will be trouble; with her father she can relax and be messy. However, she also knows her father will be furious if she ever uses any "bad words" and that her mother doesn't seem to mind at all, as long as no one else is around. Learning to live with and even enjoy the ways in which parents are different people is the beginning of learning to enjoy all the variety of people one will meet later on.

– Absence Makes the Heart Grow Fonder –

If a parent has moved far away and you hardly ever see him or her, it is amazing how wonderful they seem! The longer they are gone, the easier it is to forget the normal human weaknesses of a person. The trouble is that then it is easy to fall into a pattern of blaming everything unpleasant on the parent you live with. Also, when you do have a chance to see the parent who lives far away, it may be an awful letdown.

In your daydreams you may be remembering somebody superhuman, someone who is always kind and thoughtful, can do everything better than anybody else, and who doesn't have any faults at all. Unfortunately, there just aren't any such people, anywhere! Everybody has some special and wonderful things about them, as well as faults and weaknesses. That is a hard thing for any child to learn. When you were a little baby and couldn't take care of yourself at all, you needed to believe that your parents were always strong and wonderful. As you get older and don't feel quite so helpless, you can begin to see your parents as real human beings, with faults and limitations.

All children go through this process and sometimes it can be quite painful. It usually happens somewhat more easily when you live with both parents. When you don't see a parent all the time, it is harder because it doesn't happen quite so gradually. If a child has put a parent on a pedestal for quite some time, it can be quite a shock when he or she begins to see their imperfections.

Sometimes what happens is that the child then goes to the other extreme altogether. Alexis felt that way.

He missed his father so much that he began to think about him as if he were a great athlete or a movie star. When he visited his father after several months of being separated, he realized that his father was sometimes tired and impatient, that he seemed to have a lot of things on his mind and didn't pay much attention to him. All of a sudden Alexis began to feel very angry at his father. He wasn't so wonderful after all, and the disappointment was almost more than he could bear. When the visit was over, and when he was on the plane going home, he thought to himself, "Well, I guess I just don't really have a father anymore. He's really a jerk—he doesn't know how to treat me at all." Later, after he had a chance to think it over some more, he began to realize that his father wasn't a hero, but he wasn't a devil. He was simply a man with the same kinds of problems that most people have.

The best kinds of loving feelings are those in which we can love somebody without having to make up fairy tales about them. If we think about it, that's really the way children feel about themselves. They want their parents, their grandparents, their teachers and their friends, to love them even though they are far from perfect. Loving feelings can be even stronger after people learn to accept each other as they really are. You are a lovable person even if you aren't good at reading or multiplication. You are a lovable person even if you can't throw a baseball well. You know that the people who love you the most are the ones who love you because you are you. The time will come when you will be able to love your parents in the same way—just because they are the way they are.

— When Parents Have Special Problems —

Sometimes a divorce makes it hard for a child to remember that he or she is a child. For example, even though Penny is only nine years old, it often seems that she and her mother have switched places—that she is the mother and her mother is the child. It is frightening when Penny's mother gets very depressed and doesn't talk at all. Penny tries so hard to cheer her mother up, and she is afraid to upset her mother.

One weekend when her dad wanted her to go to the beach with him, Penny said, "I can't go—Mommy says she'll kill herself if I leave her alone." Penny's dad said, "I want you to come. You are not responsible for what your mother says or does." Penny went away with her dad, and nothing terrible happened. Her father tried to explain that her mother doesn't mean all the awful things she says; that is part of her unhappy feelings.

It is very likely that unless Penny's mother gets some help for herself, sooner or later Penny and her brother will probably go to live with her father. But

Penny is afraid of that, even more than staying with her mother. She worries a lot about her mother and she feels bad about how unhappy her mother is.

The biggest problem of all is that Penny *likes* being in charge of things. It makes her feel big and strong to be the one who takes care of her mother and brother. When her parents were first divorced, she felt so frightened that no one would take care of her. Now taking care of things helps her to feel less frightened. She has found out that she is a stronger person than her mother and in some ways that is comforting. But it is not a good idea for a child to take care of a grown-up. It is too heavy a burden for a little girl.

– Taking Control –

After the first few months, you may begin to notice that you have a lot to do with how things are going. If you come home from a visit with your dad and complain about what a lousy time you had, and how mean and inconsiderate your father was, that keeps things pretty steamed up. Or, if every time you visit your dad you give him a long list of all the rotten, mean things Mom has done that week, this is often a way of keeping a lot of fights going, just as in the beginning.

After a while most children figure out that they can help make it possible for their parents to deal more comfortably with each other, if they don't think they have to give such dramatic reports on each parent.

The truth usually is that some visits are fun, some are boring and some are unpleasant. That's pretty much the way it is at home, too. And not just for divorced families, but for all families. There are always ups and downs, good times and bad, fun and misery. When a family lives together the parents are witnesses to all these moods and can usually judge them with some accuracy. But if they only hear one side of a story, it is likely to be distorted and create more excitement than you really intended. Maybe you thought it would be nice to come home and get a little sympathy, so you told your mother all about Daddy's losing his temper. All you wanted was for your mother to feel a little bit sorry for you. Next thing you know, you seem to have started World War III!

Usually it is more helpful to let each experience with a parent belong to you, without constant reporting. Some things have to be worked out together, of course, and if one parent is actually cruel or very disturbed, of course the other parent must be told and must take responsibility for what happens to you. But most problems arise when children tattle back and forth continually. In a way it's sort of fun, to see how easy it is to get the other parent upset. "Gee, you should see what a mess Dad's apartment is! You have to push your way through last week's garbage." Or, "Mom went out four nights this week and I watched TV until midnight." These are the sort of reports that can cause more friction and conflict. It makes a child feel very powerful to be able to manipulate his or her parents this way, but in the long run it only makes life more difficult for a longer period of time.

It is often very difficult to figure out what is all right to say and what will upset a parent. Ginny came home after a weekend with her father and said, "Gee, we had a wonderful time! He was so funny and so happy, and we met a lady and all of us took a ride in a hansom cab in the park." That turned out to be the wrong thing to say because her mother ran into the bedroom, slammed the door and Ginny could hear her crying. A father can seem to be just as upset after you have visited your mother for a two-week summer vacation, and report that she is very quiet and sighs a lot and that sometimes she stayed in bed most of the day. Telling the simple truth can sometimes cause just as much upset as dramatizing a little.

These are real problems and there are no simple solutions. In general it is a good idea to make up your mind that you are going to have your own special relationship with your mother and a separate, special relationship with your father, and that unless there are very, very serious problems, you are not going to be a reporter. It is fair and sensible to say to a parent, "If you want to know more about that, you should call Daddy up yourself," or, "Mom, it spoils my day with Dad if I have to give him all your messages. I wish you would just call him up or write to him." And it is even braver and more grown up to be able to say to either parent, "Yeah, I feel sort of sad and mixed up, but I think I should try to work that out with each of you separately."

Sometimes visiting a parent gets harder instead of easier. At first you can still share all the things that happen when people live together. But as time goes by there are so many things you don't share. There seems to be more and more distance between you. Many children become frightened by this feeling of strangeness. Both parents and children wonder if they are losing touch with each other.

What this usually means is that the old relationship is ending and a new one hasn't had a chance to develop yet. But it will! You will begin to build new memories of the things you have done together since the divorce. There will be new experiences to share that are just between you two.

Some children begin to dread these visits. They seem so formal and not at all the way it used to be when you lived together. There begin to be long uncomfortable silences and both parent and child feel shy and self-conscious. This sometimes happens because both are trying to avoid dangerous subjects — such as feelings about the other parent. Sometimes it happens because there are so many things happening to each person that the other isn't sharing, it just seems impossible to even try to catch up.

One thing that often helps is to stop feeling you have to talk all the time. It's all right to read or watch a ballgame on a visit. It also helps if people stop trying to make conversation about *events* and just let each other know how they are *feeling*.

Rebecca says, "I was so worried that my father and I wouldn't have anything to talk about that every week I would make a list of subjects: the club I joined, and what I learned in social studies, and Jan's pajama party. But I'd get all through with telling everything in about ten minutes and then, what would we talk about the rest of the day? One week I was very tired and depressed and I didn't bother to make a list. I just told my father how I felt. I said I worried about whether or not we would get to be strangers, and that I felt very sad because when you get self-conscious with a parent, the other person doesn't seem like a parent anymore—just a friend or even a stranger. Much to my surprise, my father said he felt that way, too. We spent the whole afternoon just talking about our feelings, and the time went so fast, I could hardly believe it when it was time to go home!"

Most people find it easier to talk about things and events than about feelings. At least it seems that way at first. But if we can get over that first shyness or self-consciousness, talking about feelings can be a big help and make people feel much closer to each other. As a matter of fact, some children discover that they get to know their parents better than they ever did before.

Lester says, "When my parents lived together, I was usually left out of whatever they were talking about. Now that I see each of them alone, we are getting to know each other much better. I never knew that my mother was jealous of her younger sister, that she felt she wasn't as smart or as pretty. And I never knew that my dad wanted to be a professional basketball player when he was in high school, and that it almost broke his heart when he had to realize he wasn't quite good enough. These things came up when we were having sort of quiet talks, two by two. It's interesting to get to know your parents better—as people who have the same kind of feelings we kids have."

– Delayed Reactions –

Many people—both children and adults—aren't able to show their feelings while too many things are happening all at once. They get all closed up—they don't want to talk, they don't cry—they just feel numb and far away. That doesn't mean that they don't feel just as strongly as the people who are able to show their feelings very easily. It means that it takes them longer to figure out how they do feel, or that their feelings are so strong that they feel they need to hold them in until they calm down, or they will just explode. People who have delayed reactions are likely to feel worse—or at least to know they feel worse—during this later period, many months after the divorce.

— Safe Targets —

Here is a letter that a mother wrote to me. See if you can figure out the problem. The letter said:

Dear Mrs. LeShan,
I need some advice. I am having terrible troubles with my eleven-year-old daughter. I agree with you that children should be allowed to express their feelings, but where do you draw the line? Candi says terrible things to me, like "I hate your guts," right in front of other people. I don't want her to have to hide her feelings, but she is disrespectful, negative and hostile almost all the time lately. She used to be a sweet child, but now her temper is terrible.

Sincerely yours,

Mrs. M. C.

P.S. She is never like that with her father. We have been divorced for a year and he lives in a different state. Sometimes when I get desperate I threaten to tell him how she's acting, and she gets hysterical.

I wonder if you can figure out what I wrote to Mrs. M.C. Maybe you'd like to write her an answer yourself, giving her some advice, and then compare it to what I said. Do that first before you read my answer!

What I said was that it sounded to me as if Candi was having a delayed reaction to the divorce, and that a lot of the anger she was expressing toward her mother was really deep-down anger at her father. But since she didn't see him very often, and had more chance to miss him and maybe even feel deserted by him, she couldn't let him know how she felt.

Candi lives with her mom and probably feels sure her mother loves her. They have to go through everything together, and her mother has to play "the heavy" every time Candi wants to do something that her mother doesn't think she should do. But when Candi gets angry it is about twice as mad as she might ordinarily feel because at least half of her angry feelings are really at her father. But she needs him too much, and sees him too little, to ever take a chance on being nasty to him.

People often get angry at one person when they are really angry at somebody else. Our feelings need to come out, but sometimes we don't even know who or what is causing them, and we may need help to figure it out. For example, Nancy gets really angry at her older brother, but she's scared of him, so she finds an excuse to take a poke at her younger sister. That's called "finding a safe target."

This is something that happens very frequently in divorced families. Usually the parent the children live with is the one who gets all the complaints and angry words. If you think about it, it really isn't fair. If both parents still lived together, all the angry feelings wouldn't be focused on one person—unless, of course, the children felt safe with one parent and a little scared of the other parent. What we need to understand is that when we feel very angry at one parent, maybe it is because we don't want to think about how angry we are at the other parent.

– *Love and Blame* –

Bob and Dave's father has a sickness called "compulsive gambling." He bets on horse races and at card games, not just once in a while but all the time; he cannot stop himself. Before Bob and Dave were old enough to understand what was going on, their father had lost so much money on betting that he had to sell their house and car and furniture and their mother's jewelry. Bob saw his mother cry a lot when he was little, but he didn't know why. He adored his father, who was very funny and always gave him presents. He and Dave knew that as soon as their dad came home, it would be fun. He would tell them jokes and let them stay up late and he would tell them secrets they weren't supposed to tell their mother—like the time he took them to a horse race and let them each eat five hot dogs. It seemed to Dave and Bob that their father was handsome and funny and loved them a lot.

Meanwhile, their mother was getting meaner and nastier all the time, yelling and fighting with their father. When she took them away from their dad and got a divorce, they were so angry they wanted to hurt her or run away. Their mother tried to explain, but they didn't want to listen to her. All during the years they were growing up they kept on telling themselves that everything that had gone wrong was their mother's fault. They loved their father so much that they just could not let themselves look at the facts.

Now Dave and Bob are young men. They still love their father, but they know he is a sick person who cannot stop himself from gambling, and that their mother *had* to take them away. Now they know that it was their mother who really took care of them, who went to work to support them, who worried about their schoolwork and their health and who corrected them when they did anything that was dangerous or unkind.

But all the years they were growing up, they thought their father was a terrific guy and their mother was a witch. Even when months went by when their father didn't come to see them; even when he asked to take back presents he'd given them; even when he came to their apartment when they were all out and took some of their clothes and the TV and the radio—they still needed to believe that he was a great man.

Children want so much to feel that way about a parent—especially a parent they are not so sure about. An interesting thing sometimes happens: The weaker and more irresponsible and unreliable a parent may be, the more a child may hold on to the idea that the parent is perfect. If a mother or a father is really a pretty put-together kind of person, then it is easy to see their faults because they also have so many good qualities. But if a parent has a great many problems and can't really be much of a parent, that is very frightening and upsetting, and so children want to cover up some of the feelings they have deep down—they need to pretend that the parent is really fine. It hurts too much to see the serious flaws.

– *Learning More about the Divorce* –

In the beginning, when parents are first separating, it can be extremely difficult to figure out what is happening. One minute it all seems to be all Mother's fault and the next minute, all Father's fault. It may seem that the reasons for the divorce were really very silly and not important enough for all the commotion. At any rate, so much is happening all at once that it isn't easy to know just exactly what is going on.

As time passes, you will learn more about what really happened. In the beginning perhaps nobody wanted to say too much about it, but after a while, children begin to overhear conversations; grown-ups begin to be a little more careless about what they say in front of the children. When the real reasons for the divorce come out, they can hurt a lot.

Carl only knew that his parents were having terrible fights with each other before the divorce. Now he has found out that the reason was that his mother was seeing another man. That makes him feel more ashamed and angry than he was in the beginning. Donna has found out that her father took a lot of money that didn't belong to him and that there was a time when he almost went to jail. That is worse than anything that has happened so far.

The exact opposite can happen, too. Many children who are very angry at one or both parents in the beginning discover that their parents were really very brave and very sensible. Being divorced has actually made them much happier people—and therefore better parents. It certainly didn't seem possible at the beginning, but it has turned out to be much more fun to be with each parent separately. It's not a way that a child prefers, but it is certainly better than everybody feeling miserable all the time.

As time passes, one of the good things that happens is that most children begin to understand that a divorce is almost never entirely the fault of one parent or the other. Both parents have certain strengths and weaknesses, and if being married to each other turned out to be a mistake, maybe you can begin to see that the divorce was necessary in spite of what a hard thing that is to do when there are children. Maybe it happened because your parents loved you a lot and did not want you to live in a household where people were very unhappy, where it was a lie to go on trying to live together.

– Big Changes Begin Again –

One thing that many children in divorced families do feel jealous about is that children in married families don't have to wonder all the time what is going to happen next. When your parents are divorced, some-times big changes come along, just when you least expect them.

Joseph's parents have been divorced for three years. He lives with his mother and two sisters, goes to the same school, sees his father often. His parents have even learned how to be polite to each other, which certainly makes life easier. Now, quite sud-denly, two big changes are going to take place. His father is going to marry Lou-Anne, the girl friend he's had since before the divorce, and his mother has de-cided to move from Rochester, New York, to Berke-ley, California.

Joseph is even more upset now than he was in the beginning. He says, "I had just about given up any hope that my parents would get together again, and I was glad that we all lived near each other, and every-thing was going along pretty smoothly. Now my mother says she wants to stop teaching for two years and get a master's degree. She's going to sell our house and go to school for two years. I think she wants to punish my dad because he's getting married again, but she's really punishing *me*. Now I'll never get to see my father at all."

It is very common that just as children begin to feel that they are settling down and that being part of a divorced family isn't the worst thing in the world, something new happens. Sometimes you begin to have all the awful feelings you had in the beginning. It is natural this should happen. But now you know that you are a strong person and that you *do* get to feel better again. That usually helps a little.

Of course, it isn't always unpleasant things that can surprise you; sometimes they are things that could turn out to be very nice. But when you are a child and have lived through a divorce, it is natural to be afraid of more changes.

Danny and Hilda haven't seen their dad since he ran away when they were little kids. Now they are nine and eleven years old, and the truth is they think it would be great if their mother would find someone new to marry so they could have a father. Every time their mother has gone out with a different man, they have hoped their mother would fall in love. It's been a great disappointment to them when someone they really liked a lot didn't come back.

A few months ago their mother began to go out with Leon, who is also divorced and has a daughter who lives with him. Danny and Hilda liked him right away. He has a good sense of humor, and he's fun, but he can also be firm and strong if anything goes wrong. They both thought it would be great if their mother married Leon. But now that it is about to happen, it seems like an *awful* idea! Suppose he changes after the wedding? Maybe he believes in spankings! Maybe he will start fighting with their mother—maybe, just when they get to love him a lot, he will leave, the way their father did! Suppose he doesn't like to go camping? Suppose their real father came back and wanted to see them and he said "No"?

It is normal and natural to feel this way. The unknown is scary; there is no way of knowing for sure how things will work out. But if there have been good feelings, chances are it is going to work out. It is important to remind yourself that every family has problems, that everyone has good days and bad ones, and the same is going to be true for a new family.

– *When Parents Choose New Partners* –

A few months after the divorce, most children discover that each of their parents wants to meet someone new to love. Sometimes this happens quickly, other times it doesn't happen for many months. Whenever it happens, most children feel mixed up and uneasy about it. One of the reasons for this is that it makes a child feel disloyal to a parent to begin to like someone else. For example, every time Ronnie goes to visit her daddy, a lady named Kathleen goes to the movies and to restaurants with them. She's very nice and very pretty, and Ronnie can see that Kathleen is trying very hard to be friendly. But Ronnie tries hard not to like Kathleen because she feels that if she likes Kathleen she will be hurting her mother's feelings. She also worries about whether or not Kathleen might turn out to be her stepmother.

One rainy Saturday when Ronnie's father had an emergency to take care of at his office, she and Kathleen spent the day alone together. When Kathleen said, "I think you've watched enough television for today," Ronnie shouted at her, "Don't tell me what to do! You're not my mother!" In situations like this, angry feelings are natural; Ronnie doesn't want Kathleen to think she can replace her mother. What is helpful to remember is that nobody can ever take a parent's place. It is all right for Ronnie to like Kathleen, whether or not Kathleen ever marries her father.

Divorced parents both know that it is likely that sooner or later their ex-spouses will get married again. Slowly but surely they will realize that new people are probably going to be part of their children's lives. If a child can think of these new people as special friends, that can help a lot.

Sometimes a new person *does* begin to try to act like a parent too soon. If that does happen, it will probably help to talk about it right away. Maybe Ronnie might say, "I like you and you are a nice person, but I have a mother and a father and even if they don't live together, I want them to be the ones who make the rules." It is also very likely that if Ronnie and Kathleen can be patient and understanding with each other, after a while neither one will worry about who makes the rules.

These days there is one thing that often happens after a divorce that didn't happen before. Many years ago, if a father or a mother fell in love with someone new, they tried very hard to keep it a secret until they decided to get married. Nowadays many people feel that there is nothing wrong with letting children know what is happening. They want to try to be more honest and open about it. Many people who get a divorce are frightened about getting married again. They want to be very sure that they are not making another mistake. They feel that for a while at least it would be better if they tried to live together without getting married.

One day Becky's mother said, "Harry is going to come and live with us. You know we have been seeing each other quite a while, and we love each other very much. But we are not ready to get married." Becky is very upset. What will her father think about this? Will her mother tell him? Suppose her grandparents find out about this! What will her friends think if they visit overnight? Will Harry try to boss her around? The best thing is to ask these questions right away. If a parent wants you to know about something, they must also want you to understand.

Sometimes parents feel worried and embarrassed about explaining. When Jim and Hilary visited their dad, they noticed that there were things in his apartment that obviously belonged to a lady. Their dad's friend, Claire, seemed to be around most of the time, but nobody told Jim and Hilary what was going on. Finally Hilary got up her courage and said, "Jim and I think that Claire is living here when we aren't here. Is that true? We would feel better if you just explained to us what is happening."

Sometimes if a child likes the new person very much, he or she wishes that the parent would get married. It is scary to think about having a step-parent. If the new person seems nice, it is natural for a child to feel, "It had better be this one—otherwise it might turn out to be someone I don't like." But, difficult as it may be, children cannot make such decisions for their parents. It is a good idea to let parents know how you feel, but that is not the same thing as trying to force them to make a decision.

Some divorced parents need to get to know a number of different people. It is a way they learn more about themselves. It is a way of not making the same mistakes they may have made before. During the first year after the divorce, Jean's mother had three different friends. Each time it seemed as if Jean's mother might get married, but each time the relationship ended. Jean got to like each of the men a lot. When they disappeared, it really hurt. She couldn't help feeling that maybe these people went away because they didn't like *her*. It will help if Jean can say, "I feel bad about Dick not coming here anymore." Then her mother can probably explain why things didn't work out. Children are never the real reason why two people decide not to see each other again.

Sometimes someone comes along that you just don't like at all. It worries you a lot because you can't imagine having to live with someone you don't like. Before you do anything, you need to think about why you feel this way; is there *really* something awful about the person, or is it just that anybody would bother you because you still wish your parents would live together again?

It may be a good idea to just wait and see and try not to get too upset right away. When parents divorce they need to work out a lot of their problems and their feelings. They need time and they need different kinds of experiences. Sometimes they choose to see someone who is the exact opposite of the person they were married to. Your parents' good feelings about themselves are often shattered by a divorce. Sometimes they choose someone just because he or she makes them feel more self-confident, someone who builds up their feelings about being attractive or bright or warm and nice.

Tony was very upset when his father had a girl friend who was twenty years younger than his father. Later he realized that this relationship made his father feel young and attractive, and that's what he needed most, for a while.

Sharon and Vera got very upset when their mother began to see a man who was old enough to be their grandfather. After a while they realized that what their mother needed for a little while was someone who would make her feel like a little girl who had a daddy to take care of her. As parents recover from the divorce, and as they continue to learn more about themselves, they will choose a special person for more grown-up reasons.

Sometimes a parent goes on being alone for a long, long time. That can be hard for a child, too. Many children worry a lot about the parent they do not live with; they worry about this parent being very lonely. Sometimes they wonder if anybody is ever going to love that parent again.

Some mothers and fathers need a long time to recover from a divorce; they just don't feel ready to have a new relationship. A parent has a right to decide such things for him- or herself. Your parents know that if they do remarry, it will have to be someone who will be glad to have stepchildren. That is not your responsibility.

If parents and children are patient and don't get worried about everything that happens, time usually takes care of a lot of problems. In other words, don't push the panic button too soon. People have to go through stages when they have been through very painful experiences. It probably took a long time for your parents to realize their marriage couldn't work. It also takes a long time to begin to build new families. And plenty of growing time is a very good thing.

new family combinations

This chapter is mostly for the three out of every four children whose parents get married again.

I once knew a woman named Jeanette. When she was quite young she went to live with her father and her grandparents. She had a whole bunch of cousins who were stepsisters and stepbrothers to each other. When she was older, her father married a second time, so Jeanette had a stepmother. Later on she had two half sisters and one half brother. There were so many remarriages in her family while she was growing up that sometimes a cousin was also an aunt! It was a very complicated family. And also a pretty typical family, for all this started more than eighty years ago and Jeanette grew up to be my mother. New families growing out of old families, stepparents and stepbrothers and stepsisters are nothing new at all. The difference is that in earlier times more parents died and their partners remarried. Divorce was not as common as it is today.

It is important to remember that throughout history families have changed and yet children have been able to grow up and survive these situations. In most cases these new families work out rather well. Often a family finds that after a while nobody really remembers or cares how it all started and who came from where!

Of course, there are some very big differences between a parent dying and a family that gets divorced. The first big difference is that in a divorce, a man and a woman choose to be separated. The second big difference is that when each or both remarry, a child is likely to end up with three or four parents—and, for a while at least, that can be very complicated.

– When Parents Remarry –

If children are pretty grown up when their parents remarry, chances are that the new husbands and wives are likely to be special friends more than parents. The same thing is true about the person who marries the parent you don't live with most of the time.

Judy is twelve years old and lives in Chicago. Her father and his new wife live in Los Angeles, so she is only with them for Christmas and in the summertime. She doesn't really think of Fran as a stepmother—she's just a nice lady who makes her laugh a lot and in whom she can confide, as Fran can keep secrets.

Back in Chicago, there is a man who seems just like a father—her stepfather, Henry. Henry married her mom when Judy was nine years old. She lives with him all the time, except for Christmas and part of each summer. Somehow she and Henry both seemed to understand that when a child is nine years old and when she lives with her mother and stepfather, that man is going to be a father—an extra father.

When Judy got chicken pox and her mother was on a business trip, Henry stayed home and took care of her. He tells better ghost stories than anyone she ever met. He also knows how to make great spaghetti with meatballs! What is far more important, Judy knows that Henry loves her a lot. Her own dad has been so far away for such a long time that Judy and Henry almost never even think about Henry being her stepfather. She calls him Henry because it would feel funny to call two people "Daddy," but more and more lately she calls him "Pop." It started as a sort of a nickname or a joke, but the thing is that Judy likes to think of him as a father as well as a special friend.

It is easier for Judy to do this because her own father has been gone a long time and lives so far away. Christopher has had a much more difficult time. He lives with his father and his father's new wife, but he sees his mother every week. His mother comes to school to meet his teachers; she takes him shopping for all his new clothes; she helps him with his homework; she takes him on trips to visit his grandparents. When Christopher broke his leg, he stayed at his mother's apartment for three weeks so she could take care of him.

Christopher's mother has not remarried and often

seems very lonely. His mother is still angry because Christopher's father got custody of him, and now that his father has married again, his mother seems even more upset. Sometimes she is so depressed that she just goes to bed for weeks at a time. Christopher knows that the reason he lives with his father is that his mother is a person who can be very happy for a while, and then gets so sad she can't even talk to anyone. It is a kind of sickness. She has to go to the doctor a lot and take special pills. Christopher feels very close to her and he worries about her.

When his father's new wife tells him to finish his vegetable or take a bath or wash the dishes, Christopher feels angry and upset. He doesn't want Lil to think that she's his mother. He feels so upset that he can't even let her be a friend. But by the time parents begin to remarry, children usually have learned how important *time* is. Changing, getting used to new things, takes time.

– An Unwelcome Surprise –

Some things that happen can make it harder for a child to get to know a stepparent. Roger and Arthur were eight and eleven years old when their parents separated. They lived with their mother and saw their father often. They could call him and arrange a date any time they wanted to, and they were used to staying with him most weekends.

The divorce became final while Roger and Arthur

were away at camp for the summer. The day they came back there was their father with a woman they had never seen before—his new wife! He had gotten married without ever telling them anything about it, without their ever meeting Rosalind. It was a terrible shock. They were so mad at Rosalind they could hardly look at her. No matter how friendly she tried to be, as far as they were concerned she was a monster. They felt that she was a liar and a cheat to marry their father without even wanting to meet them first. For almost a month Arthur and Roger refused to visit their father or talk to Rosalind. Their mother was as angry as they were, and she agreed with their not wanting to see their father; in fact she was pretty happy about it.

One day Arthur's gym teacher asked him if anything was wrong. He said, "Ever since school started, you've really been goofing off and not helping your team at all. I get the feeling you're upset about something." Arthur told him the story about coming home from camp and finding a new and strange stepmother. The teacher said, "I can understand how you and Rog must have felt. That *was* a shock. But I wonder why you feel so angry at Rosalind. After all, she never met you and didn't know anything about your feelings. Maybe she didn't even like doing it that way. It seems to me that probably you are really much more angry at your dad. He's the one who is close to you, and he's the one you love. He is your father and he should have understood your feelings. Maybe it would be a good idea to call him up and tell him you want to see him to tell him how you feel."

Arthur was scared—his voice even trembled when he called his father. But his dad sounded so glad to hear his voice. Arthur said, "Dad, I want to talk to you—alone." They made a date to meet in his father's office after school. When Arthur got there, his father looked very glad to see him, but he seemed more nervous than Arthur. As quickly as he could before he lost his courage, Arthur blurted out, "Roger and I were really sore at you because of what you did. You hurt our feelings. You could have visited us at camp to tell us. Why didn't you want us to meet Rosalind? Isn't it important for us to like her?"

Arthur's father looked sad and ashamed. "I know it was wrong," he said. "I hope you will believe me when I tell you that Rosalind and I have both regretted the way we did it, and I have missed you and Rog so much! I was going to call you, but I thought I'd give you a little while to cool off. I waited too long. I guess I'm not as brave as you are. The trouble is that I can't tell you why we did it that way. It has to do with some legal things about the divorce. It is something between me and your mother and the lawyers. Much later when you are grown up, maybe I'll be able to explain it. You know already that the divorce was pretty terrible and that there was a lot of fighting and a lot of trouble.

"Rosalind and I have known each other for a long time. I think that when you get to know her, you will understand why I love her a lot. Do you think you could trust me enough to believe that I had a good reason for what I did to you? Or let's say, I *thought* at the time that it was the best way, but I have had plenty of time to see I was probably wrong. Most of all, I hated hurting you that way and I am terribly sorry. Will you give us another chance?"

Arthur felt so relieved that he began to cry. Then he felt ashamed of himself. It had taken so much courage to call his dad, and now he was afraid he had ruined the whole thing by acting like a baby. Then he noticed that there were tears in his father's eyes.

The next week Roger and Arthur went to see their father and Rosalind. Everyone was shy and embarrassed. Rosalind acted silly; she talked too fast and she drank too much wine and got a little drunk. When they went home, they felt a little better—but not too much. Over the next few months they gradually got to know Rosalind. They found out that she was a much calmer person than they had thought at first. She was really a quiet and sensible person. One day when they were all having lunch in the museum cafeteria, Rosalind said, "Hey, remember the first time we went to a restaurant together? I smoked a whole pack of cigarettes and drank about five glasses of wine, I was so nervous. Boy, was I ever *sick* that night!"

– Hopes and Disappointments –

Sometimes, if a parent can't seem to decide just how much he or she wants to go on being a father or a mother, that may make things more complicated.

One stepfather, who was trying very hard to learn to take care of Glen and Paul, told me, "Just when Caroline and I think we have worked things out as a family, Joe reappears. We never know when he will turn up. Months can go by when he ignores his kids completely. I can see that they are starting to accept me as a new father and then, suddenly, he shows up with all kinds of presents and great plans for things they are going to do together. The children get all excited and hope that *this time* he is really going to stay around. Then suddenly, he's off again. He doesn't write or call and the boys are so hurt and upset. They want to let me be a father to them, but Joe never gives them a chance to settle down, to know what's going to happen next."

Sometimes this happens when a parent feels very guilty. Joe is a man who found it very hard to be a husband and a father. He likes to travel and do whatever he feels like doing. Most of the time he's glad he is now living alone. Then, every so often, he begins to feel guilty and so he comes for a visit.

The same kind of thing happens with Jack's mother, Carol. She has become a painter, and she loves her new life. But every once in a while she suddenly feels very guilty because she left home when Jack was still a baby. She knows she hasn't been such a great mother. Meanwhile Jack has a stepmother, Miriam. She's almost the only mother he can remember, and he loves her a lot. For months at a time he never even remembers that Miriam is his stepmother. But then Carol comes to see him. She hugs and kisses him and cries and promises all kinds of things she's going to do with him. But it never happens. Soon she goes away and Jack feels all shaky again. Carol is very pretty and lively, and when she's around he sort of wishes he could go and live with her. Jack feels guilty about liking Carol—he's afraid it hurts his stepmother's feelings. Miriam takes such good care of him, all the time—and there he is, kissing this sort of crazy lady in the gypsy clothes who suddenly appears for a little while.

– Old Loyalties – and New Ones –

Patty hasn't seen her father for a year and a half. When her mother brought a friend home for dinner, Patty could see her mother liked Louis a lot. Patty got very mad at her mother and wouldn't talk to Louis, no matter how much he tried to be nice to her. When her mother and Louis got married, Patty made up her mind that she would never, ever, like him. She had to work pretty hard at it because he was really a nice person. He was very fair and when he said he was going to do something, he did it. He tried very hard to get to know Patty, and to love her, but Patty couldn't give him a chance.

On the face of it, this seems like a dumb way to behave, but it is not at all. Many children feel the same way. They are still grieving for the parent who has left them and they feel very disloyal getting to like someone else. "My daddy is the best in the world," Patty tells her friends, but deep down she is hurting terribly because he doesn't come to see her and doesn't answer her letters and forgot her birthday. Somehow she has the idea that if she lets herself like her new stepfather, then her own father will never come back—but that if she refuses to love anyone new, maybe, just maybe, that will bring her father back.

That idea is a natural one to have, but it is not the truth. After a while you need to begin to realize that no matter how much you may feel deserted or neglected by a parent, that parent really wants the best for you. A person may grow up unable to be a good parent and to take care of a child properly. That is a serious problem and not your fault in any way. Such a parent really wants his or her child to be happy and to be taken care of. Loving someone new doesn't mean you don't also love the parent who has left. One kind of love has a lot of sadness and pain in it, but it is still love. It will hurt less if you allow good new things to happen without feeling guilty or disloyal.

One mother, who ran away from her husband and children, told me about it several years later. She said, "I was a child myself when I got married. I didn't know what I wanted. The next thing I knew I had a husband, a house, a car and three children! My parents had taught me to believe that was all any girl had a right to want out of life. But it wasn't. I felt trapped. What I did was awful and desperate. I behaved like the child I still was, and now I feel guilty and sad about what I did. But the one thing that has helped me begin to grow up and learn about myself and understand how I need to grow up, is that I know my children are loved by, and are able to love, a second mother. I feel that I must have done something right for them because they have so much love to give other people. Sure I get jealous once in a while, and I have many regrets, but I also have peace of mind knowing the children love their new mother and were able to make that difficult adjustment very well."

As children get older, they begin to realize that they are not responsible for the ways in which parents behave. They also discover that loving one person a whole lot doesn't interfere at all with loving another person. We all love different people in different ways.

Sometimes children can even explain this to parents. As we grow up, we discover that parents have all the same kinds of feelings that children have— especially when it comes to worrying about whether someone loves you or not. Eventually, Glen and Paul were able to tell their father, "You don't have to feel bad because you can't be our full-time father. We understand." And after a while, Jack was able to say to his mother, "I like having you come to see me, and you should be happy, too, that Miriam takes such good care of me."

— Confused Feelings —

It is natural to have mixed-up feelings when parents remarry. So much has happened, that you just don't know what you think or feel about anything anymore. And the hardest part of all is that some feelings seem so silly.

Sherry has lived alone with her mother for two years. She's afraid that her stepfather will take her mother away from her and she'll be left alone. Irwin is afraid to like his stepfather too much; what if his mother and stepfather start arguing the way his mother and father did, before they got a divorce? That separation hurt a lot. Irwin is afraid to love his stepfather too much because he might lose him, too.

Sometimes you still feel very angry at a parent, blaming him or her for the divorce. But it is too frightening to let that parent know how angry you are, because you need him or her so much. Then a stepparent comes along, and you can't figure out why you hate this person so much. You just can't stop yourself; you behave in a perfectly terrible way.

What may be happening is that someone has come along whom you don't need as much, and so the anger begins to spill out—but at the wrong person.

Another thing that sometimes happens is that when a parent remarries, you get along wonderfully with that person, but begin to fight a lot with the parent you've been living with alone. This usually means that there were still a lot of angry and unhappy feelings inside, but that you didn't feel it was safe to let them out until your mother or father was happy again and had another person to lean on.

Nina figured this out one day after she and her mother had had a terrible argument about cleaning up her room. She said such mean things to her mother that her mother was almost in tears. Her mother said, "I didn't know you hated me so much." Without thinking about it, Nina said, "I feel angry at you many times, but I didn't want to hurt your feelings because you were all alone. Now that you have Bernie to love you, too, I can tell you when I'm mad."

Sometimes when a parent gets married again, the children feel very resentful toward the stepparent, and they can't figure out exactly why. It seems like a dumb way to feel, when all along they thought they wanted their parent to get married.

Dorothy and Barbara had been living alone with their father for two years. They had a lot of freedom because their father had to work long hours. They had learned to do a great many things for themselves. They were beginning to enjoy cooking and shopping and choosing their own clothes and telling their father when they wanted to go out for supper or when they were going to visit some friends overnight. They felt as if they were in charge of themselves. Once in a while, when either of them got sick, or when they wished they had someone to tell their troubles to, they imagined how it would be if their father got married, but most of the time, they liked the way things were going.

Now their stepmother, Louise, is running the household. She decides what they will have for supper and she wants to know where they are every day after school. They feel that Louise is interfering, that she is taking away their freedom and independence. That is a normal way to feel. Maybe they can help Louise understand that they have learned to take pretty good care of themselves. They will probably also discover, after a while, that it feels good to have a mother around and to go back to being able to be children who need to be taken care of, at least some of the time.

There is nothing foolish or silly about having all these different kinds of feelings. And it helps a lot when we don't feel ashamed of them. It also seems to make them go away, once we can talk about them.

– Names Can Be Important –

There is one special kind of worry that has to do with the problem of last names. It is difficult enough to find the most comfortable first name for a stepparent; last names can be even more complicated.

Brian and Faith live with their father, so there is no problem. Their last name will always be the same. But Adam and Jeremy live with their mother, and when she got married again, their last name was still Putnam, but their mother was now Mrs. Blackman. Their friends and teachers get all mixed up and it feels funny because they hardly ever see their own father. After a while, they really wanted to have the same last name as their stepfather.

What parents do about this problem often depends on the age of the children. If children are almost grown up, they usually want to keep their father's name. Very young children often don't like having a last name different from their mother's. Some children get very, very upset if parents want to change their name; they want to keep their old name. Other children wish their new daddy would adopt them so their name can be the same as his.

What seems to work out best is for parents and children to talk over all their feelings about this. Also, don't do anything for quite a while; it's a big decision, and people's feelings need lots of time to become clear.

– New Families –

One day four children were having a fight in the living room. Vivian was yelling at Franklin, "You can't boss me around—you're not even my real brother!" Marian was yelling at Bonnie, "It's none of your business what Vivian and I do—we don't belong to your mother!" Mrs. Mitchell heard them and came in from the kitchen. "I want all of you to do exactly what I tell you," she said in a very firm and commanding tone of voice. "Vivian, you go out to the porch. Franklin, you go into the kitchen. Marian, you go into the hall. Bonnie, you go into the bathroom." The children were puzzled, but they could tell that she meant business, and they each left the room very quietly, wondering what was going to happen next.

As soon as they were all out of the room, Mrs. Mitchell sat down on the couch. Then she called each child back, one at a time, and told them to give her a hug and then to sit down with her. When all the children were back, she said, "Here we are together; we are a family, and we all love each other. It doesn't make the slightest difference which door you came through to get here—the important thing is that you are *here*. I know you get angry at each other, and that's all right. But it has nothing to do with the way in which you got here."

Usually, just at the very same time that you are trying to get used to having stepparents, you also have to get used to having stepbrothers and stepsisters. That certainly is a big complication—for parents and for children! One divorced man who got married again said, "I didn't marry a wife—I married a *crowd*!"

It can certainly feel that way. And once again, as with so many other things that have happened, everybody has mixed feelings. If you are an only child, you might think it will be fun to have other children around, but then you might get jealous if your mother pays more attention to her stepchildren than she does to you. At the very same time you are feeling it will be good to have a man around the house again, you might be afraid that he will be nice to his own children and mean to you. Or you might think it will be fun to have a baby in the family, but at the same time think, "I'll bet I'm going to get stuck with baby-sitting all the time." Another child thinks, "I've always wanted an older brother," and at the same time thinks, "I bet he'll try to boss me around all the time." Or a child thinks, "It will be great to have a sister to tell my troubles to," and at the same time also thinks, "Suppose she's a mean, nasty kid who tattles a lot, or hangs on to me and never leaves me alone with my friends?"

By now I hope you know that we all have mixed feelings just about everything! I also hope you remember that it takes time for people to get to know each other and to work things out. It is just as hard to start a new family as it is to break up an old family.

Sometimes it seems to help a great deal if parents allow each of their children a long period of time to get to know each other, before they live together. But that's not always the case—it can go either way. Sometimes it can mean that problems get worked out ahead of time; other times living together is so different from visiting that there are just as many problems and surprises as if they had never met ahead of time. Either way, the first few months when a new group of people are trying to learn to live together, there are bound to be lots of worries, hurt feelings, misunderstandings, jealousies and feelings of not being treated fairly.

In some families this is a time when it often helps to have quite a few family meetings when everyone can sit down and talk about what is happening. This is also a time when some parents and children need outside help—someone to "referee" these discussions, someone with experience in helping families deal with their problems. Outside help is usually necessary in families where people are unable to talk about how they feel. In many instances, yelling and fussing and carrying on means that in this new family the children and the grown-ups like each other and trust each other enough to know that it is safe to express their feelings.

One mother told me, "Every time we get into trouble, we all learn something new. For example, I knew that I was worrying about how to be a stepparent, but it never occurred to me until yesterday that I was also worried about my children having a stepfather. Yesterday George yelled at my daughter for leaving her bicycle out all night. All of a sudden I got furious and told him not to talk to 'my child' in that tone of voice. Then he got angry at me for interfering. Later, when we talked it all over, I realized that I was worrying about whether or not George could be fair to my children. We are learning more and more about ourselves and each other, and we all feel much better after a crisis is over. The *best* thing we are finding out is that we really care about each other."

– Hurt Feelings –

However, in some families arguments are a sign of great tension; instead of getting better, the problems just get worse and worse. This is when outside help is needed. Chances are that you have already learned, during your parents' separation, that people often say things in anger that they don't really mean. It is important to remember that in a family where there are stepchildren and stepparents. Somehow the words often seem worse, and feelings get hurt more. A stepmother may cringe if a stepchild says, "I wish Daddy had never married you!" or a stepchild may feel like running away if a stepparent says, "I never thought I would have to put up with such problems when I married your father!"

Some people can hold grudges for the longest time! I know people who were so hurt by something someone said to them in anger that they don't talk to each other for years and years. It's a good idea to let yourself forgive things that people say when they are very upset. It's also a good idea to say, "I was very angry when I said that. I don't feel that way anymore, and I'm sorry."

In general, it is a good idea for people to try to let each other know how they are feeling. It is the only way they can improve how they get along and how much they understand each other. It is also the best way to work out problems. But sometimes it can make a big difference how we express a feeling we are having.

When Ellen gets angry, she yells, "I hate you, you fat old pig!" She's expressing her feelings of the moment, all right, but she's also being unnecessarily cruel. Sometimes we feel so upset that we want to hurt another person in a way that we know will really upset them the most. It isn't easy, but people can learn to express their true feelings without being cruel or saying things that will be hard for the other person to forget or forgive later on. Ellen could have said, "You're making me feel so angry and mean that I feel like saying terrible things to you!"

Once, when Angela was on a weekend visit, her stepmother got so angry that she said, "I don't want you to visit us anymore!" As soon as she said it, Babs was horrified at what she had said. Angela had provoked her by hitting the new baby, but Babs's anger made terrible words come out, words she didn't really mean.

Angela could have chosen to deal with this in several ways. She could have gone home and told her

119

mother what Babs had said, and then her mother would have called her father and there would have been a big fight. Or she could have not said anything to anyone and felt terrible and cried when she was alone. Or—and this would have been a much better idea than anything else—she could have let Babs cool down a little and then said, "I'm sorry I hit the baby, but you didn't have to hurt my feelings that much, even if you were angry at me."

Most old fairy tales are filled with cruel and terrible stepparents, and some children worry that these stories may be true. But the majority of stepparents are neither ogres nor angels. They may make mistakes, they don't always understand you and they may get impatient—but those are all things that happen to any parent.

One thing is certain; today's stepparents are trying harder to understand their role than any previous generation of stepparents. They are trying to learn more about the complicated feelings involved in this situation. But just as with any other kind of parents, there are special cases where a stepparent may be very unkind or behave in ways that show he or she is a person who is sick in their feelings. These are not the normal problems of families, in which love and anger are all mixed up together, and where daily living brings with it the same sorts of problems that exist in every family.

If you become truly frightened by a stepparent's behavior, you must certainly talk this over with your parent, or a teacher, doctor, neighbor or relative. You must not be quiet about someone who is hurting you or who does anything which seems very peculiar and not at all the way a parent usually behaves. The strange thing is that sometimes children feel that they deserve to be treated badly and so they are afraid to say anything. No child *ever* deserves to be beaten, or burned or locked up or molested in any way, by a parent or anybody else.

– It Really Is a Crowd –

In addition to stepparents and stepbrothers and sisters, there are lots of other new people who come into one's life—new aunts and uncles, grandparents, family friends. It isn't easy to get to know so many new people. It may even seem overwhelming, more than any person can handle. Just putting names and faces together or remembering how people are related to each other can be a full-time job.

Usually the best thing is not to try to do it all at once. Take it easy and don't be too embarrassed to say, "I don't remember exactly who you are," or "Would you please explain to me again how you are related to my new father?"

– Tired Feelings –

Some children feel very tired and worn out when the parent they live with remarries. They can't understand why they seem to need more sleep, why they yawn a lot in school even though they go to bed early, why they don't seem to have the energy to play baseball or swim.

If this happens to you, remember that people get just as tired from extreme feelings as they do from physical activities. So much has happened, and there are so many new things to get used to. It takes a great deal of energy to deal with feelings of strangeness and uncertainty about the future. Feeling shy, not knowing what to call a new parent, feeling uncomfortable meeting new people—this can all be very exhausting. For a while, you may need to rest a lot and spend some time alone. This is not usually the best time to push yourself too hard. Breaking apart an old family and putting together a new one is something of an "operation," and you need time to rest and to heal.

If you are having trouble in school, or are having nightmares, or don't feel like eating, or crave eating all kinds of junk foods, these problems will probably pass more quickly if you don't force yourself to be cheerful and bright-eyed and busy all the time. If you need to slump a bit for a while, that is a normal reaction to many changes in your life.

— *How Love Grows* —

Another thing in fairy stories is that everyone lives happily ever after. There is no more truth in this than in Cinderella's wicked stepmother being a real person. You certainly are not going to like *all* the new people who come into your life. You may never get to really love some of the people who become part of your family. But it is important to remember that nobody ever loves all the people in any family — and people can learn to respect each other and be kind to each other without having to love them.

Sometimes love takes a long time to grow. Ted just couldn't imagine that a time would ever come when he could love his stepbrother, Ralph. Then Ralph got bitten by a dog on the way home from school and Ted was very worried about him. Naomi was sure she would never like her stepmother's sister. But after a while Naomi realized that Aunt Edith was really a funny lady and that nobody took anything she said too seriously. Aunt Edith eventually turned out to be one of her favorite people.

Sometimes the people who make the worst first impressions on us turn out to be the people we end up liking best. Of course, it can work out the other way, too. Some people who make a wonderful first impression do not seem to be so wonderful later on.

– Other Kinds of Families –

There are many ways to be a family, and many younger parents, especially, feel quite happy and comfortable just being with lots of very good friends who care a lot about each other. Sometimes single parents may all buy a big house together and share it with other divorced parents and their children. It is a special kind of community family, where people choose to share their lives in special new ways.

Children whose parents don't get married again still feel that there are new people who come into their lives who are real members of their family. Terry was only three years old when her parents got a divorce. There were so many parents and children that were close friends and who took care of each other so well, that by the time she was seven or eight years old, she was surprised to learn that some children feel very upset about divorces. Where she lives, it seems to be a natural way of living, and she doesn't feel lonely or scared about the way she lives. Both her parents have so many friends that love her and take care of her that she feels as if she has a wonderful family, even though most of the people aren't related to each other at all. A family can really be any group of people who decide to take care of each other.

– We All Start Out as Strangers –

Whichever way parents and children decide to live, there is a lot of hard work for everyone. It is not easy to find a happy balance between doing the things you want to do and sharing your life with others. It takes a lot of practice and patience.

Ginny had a very interesting idea. She said, "You know what I think? I think that when a baby is born, that baby is a stranger to its parents and the parents are strangers to that baby. They need time to get to know each other. I think that's the way love always starts—with people who are strangers at first."

your
future

I have written a great deal about the sad and angry feelings that are part of a divorce. I have also concentrated on the problems that parents and children have. These feelings and problems are very real and very important. To some degree, they occur no matter how hard people try to avoid them.

Now I would like to add something that can be equally real and important, and that is that grown-ups are making a great deal of progress in learning how to deal with divorce. Because there are so many divorces and so many of these involve children, many people are seriously concerned about the best possible ways to help families who are living through this painful situation. Lawyers and judges are trying to find better ways to deal with the legal problems; mental-health specialists—social workers, psychologists, psychiatrists, marriage counselors—are offering more and better services to help people understand their complicated and difficult feelings; government agencies are thinking more and more about what they must do to help single-parent families; divorced men and women are starting organizations through which they can learn from each other how to deal with their feelings and their problems in daily living; television programs are beginning to deal with this subject; there are more and more books on divorce for both adults and children, and I have tried to list some of the best of these in the bibliography.

Because of all this increasing interest and concern, people are learning better and better ways to help families come through a divorce experience feeling good about themselves. Many divorcing parents are doing everything they can to get the best advice available. They know it is not a sign of weakness but of wisdom and strength to know when you need help and guidance from others.

The fact that most people who get divorced fall in love and marry again tells us something very important. It tells us that being loved and loving somebody else is still the most important thing that can happen to a person. For most people marriage is a good arrangement—the best we have ever found for both parents and children.

When Carrie's mother and father finally separated, Carrie told her best friend, "When I grow up, I am never, ever going to get married! It's terrible—and I'm never going to have any children either! I'm going to live by myself with two dogs and two cats, some goldfish and a turtle!" And that's how Carrie felt for a long time. But when her mother remarried three years later, Carrie began to change her mind. She liked Fred from the first time Mom brought him home. He was a quiet and kind man, and he made her feel safe and warm; she just had a feeling that he really knew how to take care of them. Carrie's mother began smiling and singing a lot; suddenly it was as if bright sunshine was all over the house. Maybe falling in love and getting married weren't so bad, after all.

One of the main reasons why there are so many divorces these days is not because people think there is anything wrong with being married, but rather that they have discovered they may be married to the wrong person. When Jerry's father remarried he told Jerry, "I was sort of a dumb kid when your mom and I got married. Now I think I'm a more serious person, and I have learned a whole lot these past few years. I think being married is a good way to be."

Some people think that the increasing number of divorces is leading to a general attitude that marriage isn't a very good arrangement. Nothing could be farther from the truth. The large majority of divorced men and women want to remarry. They feel they have learned a great deal about themselves and about how to make a marriage work. Many of them were divorced because their standards for marriage were so high, not because they have given up on the idea of marriage.

Most grown-ups who have been divorced do learn a great deal about how to make a marriage work. One mother said, "If I remarry, it will be out of strength, not out of weakness. I was really helpless and silly and very dependent when I was first married. I feel I am a truly grown-up person now. If I got married again it would be knowing how much I would have to contribute, not just finding someone to lean on." A father said, "Now I know how to cope with the unexpected. The first time I married, I had a blueprint; everything would work out just as I had planned. Now I know how silly that was. Nobody can predict the future. I'm ready to take one step at a time—to grow and change a little bit each day."

It is very likely that living in a divorced family, you already have some pretty good ideas about what it takes to make a marriage work. You realize that people ought not to get married until they are truly grown-up—that is, until they know who they are and what they need; until they have learned how to understand themselves and share their feelings openly and honestly. You can see that it takes a lot of patience, understanding and sympathy for people to love each other and live together. You know that mature people do not take having children lightly—they know that becoming parents is a serious business and demands the very best of them.

When people respect themselves and feel good about themselves, when they understand their own needs and are able to care very deeply about another person without needing to make up a fairy tale about living happily ever after, they can *work* at being married; they can make a wonderful adventure of marriage and parenthood. For most grown-ups, it still seems to be the best way we know for people to love each other and to share their lives.

Someday, many years from now, most of you will want to marry. And it is very likely that you will have learned how to make it work. To love and to be loved so much that you want to share your life with someone else is still something wonderful to look forward to.

further reading

Blue, Rose. *A Month of Sundays*. New York: Watts, 1972.

Blume, Judy. *It's Not the End of the World*. New York: Bradbury, 1972.

Caines, Jeanette. *Daddy*. New York: Harper, 1977.

Dragonwagon, Crescent. *Always, Always*. New York: Macmillan, 1984.

Gardner, Richard. *The Boys and Girls Book about Stepfamilies*. New York: Bantam, 1982.

Hazen, Barbara. *Two Homes to Live In: A Child's Eyeview of Divorce*. New York: Science Press, 1978.

Helmering, Doris. *I Have Two Families*. Nashville, TN: Abingdon, 1981.

Klein, Norma. *Taking Sides*. New York: Pantheon, 1974.

Krementz, Jill. *How It Feels When Parents Divorce*. New York: Knopf, 1984.

Mann, Peggy. *My Dad Lives in a Downtown Hotel*. New York: Doubleday, 1973.

Newfield, Marcia. *A Book for Jodan*. New York: Atheneum, 1975.

Norvelet, Matilda. *Daddy Isn't Coming Home*. Grand Rapids, MI: Zondervan, 1981.

Purcell, Margaret. *A Look at Divorce*. Minneapolis, MN: Lerner, 1977.

Perry, Patricia and Lynch, Marietta. *Mommy and Daddy Are Divorced*. New York: Dial, 1978.

Rofes, Eric, ed. *The Kids Book of Divorce: By, For and About Kids*. New York: Random, 1982.

Roy, Ron. *Breakfast with My Father*. New York: Clarion, 1980.

Schuchman, Joan. *Two Places to Sleep*. Minneapolis, MN: CarolRhoda, 1979.

Thomas, Ianthe. *Eliza's Daddy*. New York: Harcourt, 1976.